# PERSECUTION:
# IT WILL NEVER HAPPEN HERE?

By Jan Pit

Foreword by Brother Andrew

Open Doors with Brother Andrew
P. O. Box 2020
Orange, CA 92669

# CONTENTS

# FOREWORD

I recently returned from visiting a number of Central American countries. There I had the privilege of meeting many spiritual leaders. I asked each one of them in these threatened nations, "Are *you* ready for revolution, change of power, closure of churches and Bible Societies? Also the expulsion of missionaries, as well as the murder, imprisonment or immobilization of your own pastors?" Before they could reply, I also posed these further questions: "Are *you* now ready to not be able to evangelize children and young people? To work without literature and foreign funds?" Almost invariably the answer was, "No, we are not ready." Yet all the signs of imminent persecution are there for all to see in these countries.

"Be prepared" is the motto of the Boy Scout movement. This is what this book is all about. My friend and colleague Jan Pit has written a compelling work, easy to read, gripping, full of insight and truth; a book that can save your life and the life of your church. I therefore dare to say it could save the life of your country, or at least greatly help to change the course of events.

*Time* is definitely against us;

time is running out;

time is *not* going to be produced any more, and the little there is left is mainly at the disposal of the powers of darkness. Both the Bible and the newspapers tell us this.

Here's a book that follows the Scriptures and tells us plainly how to redeem the time in which we live — the time in which we see the devil's first attack on a worldwide scale to wipe out the Church of Jesus Christ. It is probably his last attack too, but he will *not* win. The question is: will *you* win? Or even survive? And how about your church?

This book will greatly help you. It will be a *life*-saver; it is a *must*.

It is, to my knowledge, the only book on this subject — *not* on how to survive, but how to conquer in the face of an overwhelming enemy, the strongest force God's creation has ever encountered.

Let this book become our "manifesto." It will unite us and make us *more* than conquerors through Him who loved us and gave Himself for us — as Jan Pit, other Open Doors workers and myself give ourselves for the Suffering Church.

*Brother Andrew*
Post Office Box 47,
*ERMELO*
Holland.

# Chapter 1

# "IT WILL NEVER HAPPEN HERE"

"Will passengers leaving on Flight 109 please proceed to Gate 12." As if in a daze I walked towards the gate and onto the airplane for my first-ever flight. Would it be all right? How could such a monster as this wing heavenward, let alone stay in the air?

As I settled in my seat I could see that the plane was completely full. One stewardess was handing out newspapers and candy, while another called for our attention on the loudspeaker.

"Good afternoon, ladies and gentlemen, and welcome aboard." Again a soothing voice that was meant to alleviate all panic. "Your stewardess will now demonstrate the use of the oxygen mask."

Chills ran up my spine as the smartly-dressed "flying waitress" pulled out something that looked like a gas mask and went through her well-rehearsed mime.

"In the unlikely event of the loss of cabin pressure, a panel directly above your head will open automatically. If this should happen, please pull the mask down towards you and place it over your nose and mouth and breathe normally."

The horror wasn't over yet. We were then told to study a pamphlet which was to be found in a pouch attached to the back of the seat in front. It gave information on what to do in the event the aircraft plunged into the sea.

"You will find your life jackets under your seats." By now my hands were sweating and my throat was dry with panic.

Suddenly there was a terrific roar from the engines as we began shooting down the runway. Gradually gravity was defied and we were soaring heavenwards. I sat near the window, just over the wing. Once we were well in the air I glanced out and shuddered. As the plane banked, the end of the wing appeared to flap as if it would break off at any second. The stewardess' words echoed in my ears, "In the unlikely event of...." But nothing seemed to be unlikely anymore.

My maiden flight was a nightmare. I never closed an eye. Suddenly I could no longer hear the sound of the engines. "*Here we go.* We are going to crash," I thought. My mouth clammed up and I gripped the arm rests tightly. I swallowed nervously and my ears popped. Once again I heard the engines. Maybe I would survive after all.

## Persecution . . . Improbable?

Now, many years and innumerable flights later, I have grown accustomed to the flying, the grim instructions and the "flapping" wings. The instructions of the stewardesses, however, have always remained the same. "In the unlikely event of...." Those five words still retain that note of menace for me.

While reading this book you may experience a similar feeling of threat. "Preparation for persecution!" That sounds ominous. "Preparation for heaven" sounds much better, for who wants to prepare for persecution? Yet the threat is real, and the words, "In the unlikely event of ..." do not apply to the contents of this book. The Bible says persecution is certain. It is not unlikely, not even likely, but it is *certain.* Second Timothy 3:12 clearly states, "All who desire to live a godly life in Christ Jesus will be persecuted."

Is there hope? Do we have to be defeatist? No, we must not view persecution in the light of defeat, but in the light of victory. Persecution is the mark of true discipleship. There lies the hope.

Of course we know about persecution. The Book of Acts tell us much about it. The terrible persecution that occurred during the time of Nero, the Roman butcher, is well-known, as are the examples of persecution in the history of the Church. Stakes, guillotines, concentration camps in Siberia, killer prisons in Uganda, and murdered missionaries around the world bear witness to persecution. The courage displayed by martyrs in the face of death speaks clearly of victory and faith.

The mistake we make is in thinking that *we will never suffer* persecution. We are eager to apply the words, "In the unlikely event of ..." to our own situation. Yet the events in other countries ominously foreshadow what will happen in our own country.

## A Painful Question

On one of his trips to Eastern Europe, Brother Andrew, the founder of Open Doors, met a church leader who had been imprisoned many times. This preacher asked Andrew if Christians in his own country were persecuted.

Brother Andrew laughed. "No," he replied, "Christians are not persecuted in my country."

"Do they not put anyone into jail for their faith?" the man asked, a hint of disbelief in his voice.

"No, no one."

"Why not?" the preacher wanted to know.

"Because we have religious freedom in our land," Brother Andrew explained.

But the Eastern European believer insisted, "Then what do you do with 2 Timothy 3:12 where it says that godly believers *will* be persecuted?"

A painful question if you do not know the verse! Brother Andrew read it shamefacedly and then said quietly, "Nothing. We do nothing with that verse."

Yes, what do we do with this verse and the others which speak of persecution? Do we ignore those which do not fit into our plans, or do we interpret them as not applying to Christians today? We are very good at claiming the Lord's promises and ignoring the conditions. "The commandments were meant for the Israelites, not for us, for we are no longer under the Law but under the dispensation of Grace," we say. Finally, after ignoring that which we do not like, we are left with a thin Bible, containing only the promises.

We cannot change the Bible to suit ourselves, however. It clearly presents problems and conditions together. In fact, it is remarkable that most of the promises we love to quote as encouragements are conditional. We have to learn to read the Bible in this context.

One particular verse we are so fond of reading in this way is Philippians 3:10. The first part is very familiar to us: "That I may know him and the power of his resurrection ..." But it does not stop there, and few of us know the second part: "and may share his sufferings ..."

Many Christians underline certain Bible texts, and that is good. Do we, however, only underline the promises, not the commandments or conditions? One can even buy "promise boxes" containing Bible verses printed on cards. I received one of these as a gift. Printed on the outside was: PRECIOUS PROMISES. On each card was a promise — for times of sorrow, loneliness, illness, etc. No terms of fulfillment were given, just the promises. It all sounds very comforting, but it can be dangerous. Should you refer to any one of these verses in the Bible, you will always find a condition attached. The Bible is very clear: God's promises are yours and mine only if the conditions are fulfilled.

The reluctance to believe that we will not experience persecution stems from being unwilling to pay the price of discipleship. Most evangelical work is based on promises and not conditions. The excuse given is, "You will frighten people off if you tell them about the conditions."

## Your Heart Is in Your Purse

At an evangelistic campaign a preacher belabored a point: that the listeners' possessions ought to be given to God. An attractive and smartly dressed lady approached him afterward.

"Why do you speak so much about my purse and so little about my heart?" was her question. Triumph glistened in her eyes as she felt she had put him in his place.

Gravely he looked at her. "Because, madam, that is where your heart is."

Her eyes flashed. "I do not appreciate your joke," she said angrily as she flounced away.

No, such jokes (read: truths) are not appreciated. They

do not fit in with our faith. Neither does persecution. That is why we push it away to remote Communist lands like Albania, China or Russia.

"It will never happen here," we say.

But how can we be so sure? Of course we would prefer it didn't, so we can continue our cheap Christianity. But if we want to experience God's promises, we must fulfill his conditions. If we want to "overcome," we will have to accept strife. Without strife there is no victory. Remember these words from the Bible: "If my people . . ." (condition), "then will I . . ." (promise).

The Apostle Paul wrote, "I have fought the good fight, I have finished the race, I have kept the faith. Henceforth there is laid up for me the crown of righteousness . . ." (2 Timothy 4:7-8).

"I have kept the faith." When Jesus Christ refers to His second coming, He asks, ". . . when the Son of man comes, will he find faith on earth?" (Luke 18:8). This implies that many will fall away from the faith. There will be many reasons: "love of the world" (2 Timothy 4:10) or fear of persecution. "As for what was sown on rocky ground, this is he who hears the word and immediately receives it with joy: yet he has no root in himself, but endures for a while, and when tribulation or persecution arises on account of the word, immediately he falls away" (Matthew 13:20-21). Others will fall away because they love money and possessions more than Christ (Matthew 13:22).

Jesus' question, "will he find faith on earth," points to vital, personal faith, not a nominal one. When Christ comes again He will find many types of faith, but only personal faith will be a saving faith. "Even the demons believe — and shudder" (James 2:19). The faith spoken of in Luke 18:8 relates to those who are prepared to pay the price of discipleship. It is the faith that is steadfast despite persecution.

## The Lesson of Vietnam

It is not only laymen who convince themselves that persecution will not come; church leaders and missionaries have also been of the opinion that this horror would not happen in their countries.

During the appalling Vietnam war, church leaders from a certain Christian group held their annual conference. The southern Vietnamese city they were in resembled a fortress. There were soldiers everywhere, barricades, and a terrifying collection of weaponry. Daily attacks were being made on the city by the Communist Viet Cong, yet the pastors continued to discuss the various activities which they would embark upon in the ensuing years. They even adopted a ten-year plan. Despite all the evidence, no one there thought it possible for South Vietnam to be overthrown. All were convinced the country would remain open to mission work.

What happened? South Vietnam fell — not ten years later, but ten days after the conference. The leaders there in July 1976 had no insight into the situation. "It will never happen here," was their opinion. But ten days later they had to flee Vietnam.

The Church remained — unprepared.

In 1965, my wife Liese and I joined a group of missionaries in the mountainous, humid and densely forested land of Laos, once known as *Lan Xang*, "land of a million elephants." We soon found ourselves in the center of a bloody war which had erupted in Buddhist Laos after 1954 when, after being part of French Indo-China for 50 years, it became an independent constitutional monarchy with a royal capital at Luang Prabang. Efforts to form a neutral government had broken down in 1960 and a war between Royal Lao forces, supported by the United States, and the Pathet Lao, backed by North Vietnam, became a key part of the bigger conflict in Vietnam. This was mainly because of supply trails running through Laos.

So I shouldn't really have been surprised when we arrived that the first words we received from the other missionaries were, "Don't unpack. You might have to leave any day."

I now say with great shame that, although we could see that the writing was on the wall for Laos, we had no strategy for building a strong indigenous church. I remember being told by one missionary, "Jan, you may not be in this country for long, so lead as many people to Christ as you can." It was as if he were saying, "The salvation of the Laotian people depends on the presence of us missionaries."

What we should have been doing was instructing the Laotian Christians on how to evangelize their own people, instead of thinking we should do it all. We seemed to think that the Holy Spirit could only use missionaries to bring people to Christ. What arrogance we had!

The futility of thinking this way was soon brought home to me forcefully when I began to study the Laotian language in the city of Khammaouane, where we were based. It is an incredibly difficult language to master because, like Chinese, it is a tonal language with about seven different tones to it. I spent the first two years trying to cope with this seemingly impossible tongue. Many times I doubted my calling to Laos.

One day I became so depressed about my lack of progress that I turned to Liese and said, "Darling, let's go back to Holland. At least there we can talk with people who know what we are saying."

Despite the anguish I went through, the Lord still kept me there. Then came the big day when I was to preach my first sermon in a Laotian church. I had written out every word of what I considered a scintillating message and even checked it with my language teacher, a Laotian believer. He corrected the mistakes for me and when I stood to deliver it to a packed church I confidently read it to the congregation, who listened attentively. After twenty minutes, I concluded and sat down. A feeling of real achievement washed over me. I was really satisfied that at last I had communicated Jesus to the Laotians.

"How did I do?" I asked another missionary after the service.

The man looked at me with a real embarrassment.

"Brother Jan," he said, trying his best not to hurt my feelings, "they didn't have a clue what you were talking about."

"What?" I was stunned. "But my teacher checked it over before I preached."

"Yes, brother, that might have been so, but you used the wrong tones for the words. That completely changed their meaning. Not one person knew what you were talking about."

It was at that humiliating moment that I realized that we missionaries were completely wrong in thinking that we were the important ones — the only people who could win the natives to Christ. How could I personally reach those out in the villages with the message of salvation, when I couldn't even make myself understood in the first pew of the church? I was like a helpless baby.

I eventually partly mastered the language, but still couldn't communicate to the people as a native would. Instead of trying to do it all, missionaries should have trained the local Christians better. We should have taught them how to evangelize and prepared them for the certain persecution that awaited them.

We never worked under the leading of the Laotian church. We felt we knew best. But did we? When Laos fell, the missionaries left, and the Church stayed behind — *UNPREPARED*. We could flee the country because we had passports, money, friends on the outside. But what about the thousands of Laotian believers who had become reliant on us missionaries? They had no escape and little preparation from us — from *me* — to stand on their own feet.

Are we willing to learn a lesson from Vietnam or Laos? Already events similar to those I've mentioned in Asia are happening elsewhere. The revolution has swept over many countries, particularly Africa: Angola, Ethiopia and Mozambique are now under Marxist rule. Missionaries and Christians are being imprisoned and murdered by Marxist-indoctrinated terrorists. "Away with Jesus" is their slogan. The Church is persecuted and suffers.

A German missionary stationed in Ethiopia for many years wrote, "We did everything we could in Ethiopia. We built schools and hospitals. We held conferences and leadership courses. We trained church leaders for pastoral duties. We forgot one thing: to tell leaders and their congregations how to function under persecution. I am back in Germany. I cannot return to Ethiopia. The church has remained behind . . . unprepared."

## Skyscrapers and Church Buildings

After his exile from the Soviet Union, Alexander Solzhenitsyn, the famous Russian author, asked, "Are we prepared to learn from the past? Are people living in freedom able to learn from those living in need? Can the lesson they have learned be taught to the free world? Yes, it can, but who wants to learn? Our proud skyscrapers point heavenward and they say: It will never happen here. But *it will happen.* The revolution will come. Tragically, however, the free West will only believe it when it is no longer free. To quote a Russian proverb, 'When it happens you will know it is true, but then it is too late.' "

Yes, our skyscrapers and our beautiful churches point skyward as if to say, "It will not happen here." It can happen and, according to the Bible, it *will* happen.

Moreover, your land could be next. The Bible indicates persecution will be worldwide. Will we be prepared?

Many Christians maintain that we need not be overconcerned about future events, since God will give us the grace when that day arrives. Indeed, God will give us grace and help us when persecution comes. The Holy Spirit will impart power in times of need. "Have no anxiety about anything" (Philippians 4:6).

Yet we must be watchful and be prepared. The message of the Bible is clear enough. We must strive, offer resistance and overcome. The latter part is the most important.

Although persecution will increase, victory is a certainty. This was achieved through Christ. He triumphed over the powers of darkness (Colossians 2:15). We are able to face the future because of His victory. We will triumph if we put on the whole armor of God (Ephesians 6:10-11).

## Is There Hope?

Jesus once said, "You are Peter, and on this rock I will build my church, and the powers of death shall not prevail against it" (Matthew 16:18).

"Who shall separate us from the love of Christ? Shall tribulation, or distress, or persecution ... or sword? ... No, in all these things we are more than conquerors through him who loved us. For I am sure that neither death, nor life ... nor things present, nor things to come, nor powers ... nor anything else in all creation, will be able to separate us from the love of God in Christ Jesus our Lord" (Romans 8:35-39).

Strife, oppression and persecution are mentioned here. The church of Christ will not be spared, but the outcome is sure. Nothing will separate us from the love of God. That is the hope of the Church.

Is there hope for our countries too? Will God not judge the people when sin and unrighteousness are on the increase and when the love of many Christians grows cold? Yes, there is hope. The judgment of God will come to every land, unless God's people repent. "If my people who are called by my name humble themselves, and pray and seek my face, and turn from their wicked ways, then I will hear from heaven, and will forgive their sin and heal their land" (2 Chronicles 7:14).

The meaning is clear. Judgment from God can be averted. It depends on God's people. His people are called to repentance. This is not directed in the first instance to the unconverted but to the converted. They must turn from their wicked ways. Then God will heal their land. Nominal Christianity, legalism and religiosity have to give way to genuine faith.

The future of our countries does not depend on the number of *sinners* but on the number of *righteous* people. This is seen from the events which took place in Sodom and Gomorrha. The future of those cities depended on the number of righteous people and not on the number of sinners.

God saw the sins of Sodom and Gomorrah and wanted to destroy those cities. He could no longer look upon their sin. The inhabitants lived in a godless manner. The Lord's name was never mentioned except as a curse. God had decided to destroy the city. He first discussed the matter, however, with his servant Abraham. He would not pass judgment until He had talked it over with His child. God always works this way. The Church of Christ is the deciding factor in times of God's judgment.

While the Lord's messengers were on the way to Sodom, Abraham was beseeching the Lord, " 'Wilt thou indeed destroy the righteous with the wicked? Suppose there are fifty righteous within the city, wilt thou then destroy the place and not spare it for the fifty righteous who are in it? Far be it from thee to do such a thing . . .' And the Lord said, 'If I find at Sodom fifty righteous in the city, I will spare the whole place for their sake' " (Genesis 18:23,24,26).

God will do this for our country. God's people are responsible. His Church will be the deciding factor when judgment comes worldwide. While Christians are calling the godless to repentance, God calls the Christians, you and me, to introspection and contrition. Then God will spare the whole place — for our sake!

When God judges our countries and our people, will He find enough righteous people to save each nation? It depends on you and me.

Chapter 1

## POINTS FOR PERSONAL REFLECTION

1. Noah prophesied judgment, but people paid no attention. Would our reactions be the same as theirs? (Genesis 6 and 7; Matthew 24:37-39)

2. Peter did not believe Jesus should suffer. Why did he have difficulty in accepting such a possibility? (Matthew 6:21-23)

3. Peter denied his faith shortly after affirming just the opposite. Why would he be so changeable?

4. What is the application of I Thessalonians 5:1-11 to us in our situation?

## Chapter 2

# BIBLICAL PRINCIPLES OF PERSECUTION

Persecution reveals who the true followers of Christ are. Nominal Christians will fall away. Only dedicated believers will remain faithful to their Master, even unto death.

In stories about martyrs, the remarkable fact is how they faced death with great courage. They looked upon persecution as an honor and not as punishment. Acts 5 depicts this clearly. The apostles were arrested and thrown into jail. Their crime? Preaching the gospel and healing the sick in the name of Jesus. During the night an angel set them free, charging them not to go into hiding but to continue preaching the gospel. This they did the following morning. A second arrest followed. At the trial they were asked why they did not go home and keep quiet about Jesus.

"We must obey God rather than men," Peter answered.

The Jewish leaders could not misconstrue those words. It was a straightforward rejection of the established religious leaders. No wonder they were enraged and wanted to kill the disciples. Gamaliel, however, was used by God to prevent this.

Instead of being killed they were "only" beaten. They left the council with bleeding backs, "rejoicing that they were counted worthy to suffer dishonor for the name" (Acts 5:41).

Persecution was familiar to the disciples. They knew that persecution was part and parcel of their Christian walk. They knew the biblical principles. Their Master had prepared them: "A servant is not greater than his master. If they persecuted me, they will persecute you" (John 15:20). A friend of Jesus will automatically be an enemy of the world.

"If you were of the world, the world would love its own; but because you are not of the world ... therefore the world hates you" (John 15:19). Christ makes no exceptions. Nowhere does He say that some Christians will be persecuted and some will not.

## Death of Anglican Archibishop

The last hours of Janani Luwum, the Anglican Archbishop of Uganda, are a moving example of the courage of a modern-day martyr. Just minutes before he was brutally shot through the mouth at point blank range by Idi Amin, he was still caring for his "flock."

The last believer to see Luwum alive was James Kahigiriza, the then chairman of the Uganda Land Commission. Kahigiriza had also been arrested in February 1977, apparently for his friendship with the Archbishop.

He was handcuffed and confined to a stinking basement cell at the infamous State Research Bureau headquarters at Nakasero, Kampala, where thousands of Ugandans, many of them Christians, were savagely killed by Amin's "gestapo."

Kahigiriza described the situation to me. "This cell was about eight feet by eight feet. In there we were given our first meal. It was about 4:00 p.m. and as the guards began to serve food, a number of people were also brought and pushed into the cell.

"I turned around to see who they were, and to my amazement I saw one of them was my Archbishop, Janani Luwum. I noted he was wearing dark grey trousers and a black shirt; he was shoeless and both of his hands were handcuffed. He was still standing there in a state of shock when a young man in plain clothes slapped him hard on the cheek.

" 'Who are you?' the man asked harshly. 'I am the Archbishop of Uganda,' Janani replied. Immediately another guard, by the name of Kabuye, hit him again. Janani said to these men, 'You are hitting me, but I am innocent and I have done nothing. You are hitting me because you have power, but you would not have this power if it had not been given to you from God.'

"They ordered him to sit down and brought a plate of food for him to eat, which he could not do because of his broken jaw. I felt so sick because of his treatment that I could not eat either. In fact most of those men in the cell sent back their food, even though they were starving."

The grey-haired Kahigiriza then asked his Archbishop if he would offer a word of prayer.

"He prayed for all of us. It was very moving," recalled the Ugandan believer.

"After a few minutes, the Archbishop was called to come out of the cell. He was then told to put on his shoes and I thought he was about to be released.

"He came back in his full robes as archbishop, and when I saw him like that my faith was really strengthened. I felt that if he was to die, he was not going to die like any other person, but as a personal representative of Jesus Christ."

Eventually Luwum and two other prisoners, Lt. Col. Erinayo Oryema, Minister of Land and Water Resources, and Charles Oboth-Ofumbi, the Minister of Internal Affairs, were called out.

Cell-mate Apollo Lawoko, who was imprisoned for 196 days in the basement of Amin's infamous Kampala death chamber, tells of what happened to the Archbishop and the ministers after they left the cell.

"Six of us, including those three, were taken upstairs to the office of Farouk Minawa (the head of the Bureau) where Amin was waiting," he says. "We had all been seriously beaten."

Lawoka says that Amin ordered only the Archbishop and ministers into Farouk's office. "We could hear Amin accusing them, saying 'I know you were planning to kill me, to overthrow my government,' and we could hear their denials. We heard beatings with what sounded like big whips. After eight or ten minutes we heard some shots. We were hurriedly taken back downstairs and the guards warned us that if we ever spoke about what was happening upstairs we'd be skinned alive."

Shortly afterwards, Lawoko says, another guard came. "He told us the 'sheik' of the Church of Uganda and the two ministers were dead and our turn would come next day."

My colleague Dan Wooding was able to piece together for his book, *Uganda Holocaust* (co-authored with Ray Barnett), what happened that fateful day. Luwum sat on the sofa opposite the President and the Archbishop would not be cowed as they sat face to face.

"You have prayed for peace in Uganda," Amin screamed. "It shows something was going to take place. You knew there was going to be bloodshed in Uganda."

Luwum said calmly: "I have always prayed for peace in Uganda."

But the Archibishop would not admit to something that was not true. "I have nothing to do with the arms and I say once again, I am not involved."

"We were led to your house. You preached that God should save the people of Uganda from bloodshed," said the president.

During the interrogation, the Archbishop refused to sign a confession, and was ordered to lie on the floor. His cassock was pulled up and two soldiers in turn whipped him. After the beating, Luwum began praying quietly, his words barely a whisper. This was the final straw for Amin, who was so incensed that he shouted angrily and wildly, using obscene language, and he struck the Archbishop. Then he bellowed at an Acholi soldier in the room — he came from the same tribe as the Archbishop — to "kill him; kill him." The shaking soldier aimed his gun and shot the Archbishop in the groin. With that, Amin drew his pistol and fired into Luwum's face. The shot hit the Archbishop in the mouth as he was lowering his head and turning sideways. Amin's guards rushed into the room, training their rifles on Oryema and Oboth-Ofumbi. Amin, suddenly shocked by what he had done, went over to the telephone and told someone at the other end of the line, "I have lost my temper. I have shot the Archbishop. Do something."

Janani Luwum's courage in the face of death strengthened the believers.

The body of fifty-two-year-old Janani had been taken by Amin's henchmen to Mucwini, his home village, a cluster of grass-thatched mud huts, set in the middle of arid savannah plains dissected by river beds. At her homestead, his mother told the soldiers: "My son is a Christian. He cannot be buried here; he must be buried in the graveyard of the local church."

So the soliders took the coffin to the picturesque tiny hilltop church for a hurried burial. Veteran British missionary Mildred Brown was working in the region translating the Scriptures into Acholi for the Bible Society. "The soldiers had begun to dig the grave, but hadn't been able to complete the job before dark because the earth was so hard," she explained. "They left the coffin in the church overnight, so they could finish the grave the next day."

Thus the hardness of the ground gave the group of courageous believers at Mucwini the chance of gazing for the last time on their Archbishop. Many of them had watched him grow up into maturity as a Christian leader of outstanding quality.

Miss Brown continues with her account, "While the casket was in the church, the group took off the lid, first to make sure it was their beloved Archbishop, and also because they did not believe the story of the 'accident.' "

The funeral was held the next day at the village, seventy miles from the northern center of Gulu. "The church was full," recalls the Rt. Rev. Gideon Oboma, Assistant Bishop of Northern Uganda. "The people were not afraid of the danger and were even preaching to the soldiers. They had said to themselves, 'If this is to be the time of death, let us also die. But if this is to be the time to stay and live on, this will be a strong Christian witness.'

"And witness they did. For one whole month, a group of believers kept vigil at the unmarked grave, over which they put a grass cover.

"They sang and thanked God for Janani's life. They even slept in the open. Day and night they stayed at the grave, with local Christians bringing food and drink to sustain them."

And while these brave men and women were risking their lives in memory of their beloved Archbishop, the government-controlled newspaper, *Voice of Uganda*, published a call for President Amin to be made emperor and then proclaimed Son of God.

## Persecution in Iran

Idi Amin was a Muslim, and much of his killing of Christians in Uganda was financed by Muslim nations. Now, more and more persecution of the church will come from the fanatical followers of Islam. Already this is evident in Iran. Hardly had the Ayatollah Khomeini taken over the reigns of power in February 1979, when Aristo Sayeh, the Anglican vicar in Shiraz, was found with his throat slit. The crime has not been solved.

A few months later, Muslim authorities seized an Anglican hospital and a school for blind children in Isfahan. Ever since they have been intimidating believers to lead them to a supposedly missing cache of money.

One night in October 1979, two gunmen burst into the Isfahan bedroom of Anglican Bishop Hassan Barnaba Dehqani-Tafti and his British-born wife Margaret, spraying them with automatic-pistol fire. Four bullets pierced the pillow near the bishop's head. Amazingly, he was not hit, although his wife received a bullet in the arm. The bishop, president of the Central Synod which includes all Anglicans in the Middle East, fled to exile in Cyprus.

The bishop's English secretary, Jean Waddell, remained behind, and on May 1, 1980, a team of gunmen entered her apartment in search of another Anglican clergyman. First they began to strangle her, then fired two shots into her chest. She was seriously injured. Only a week later, the bishop's son Bahram, 24, was murdered with shots in the head and chest.

The Koran advocates tolerance for Christians as "People of the Book." Beyond that, the nation's new Islamic constitution guarantees freedom for both religions. So why are Muslims trying to eradicate Christian believers from their country?

Margaret Dehqani-Tafti, wife of the Iranian bishop, supplied the answer. "Most of our members are Muslim converts."

## Persecution Within the Family

Oppression can occur in several ways. It may come from a political or religious faction, but also from your own loved ones. I am reminded of a particular family. Every other day the father would stagger home drunk. His behavior caused a lot of unhappiness. When he was in this state, he would invariably row with his wife. She would suffer much abuse and often, in a blind rage, he would beat her. Naturally all this had an adverse influence on the children.

The bad example had a not surprising result. Two of the sons followed in the father's footsteps, while the rest stayed at home with their mother. The two boys would arrive home together with the father in an inebriated state. It doesn't need much imagination to guess the heartbreaking results.

One day the eldest son came to know Jesus as his Savior. A radical change took place in his life. Instead of frequenting the nearest public bar, he would go to church. At home he testified of his new life in Christ in both word and deed. He was mocked and called a weakling by his drunkard father, who no longer gave him his weekly pocket money. "You don't need it now that you no longer drink," his father informed him as he handed over his share to the brother who still drank. "At least he can buy himself an extra drink with this," the father added in a contemptuous tone.

At meal times the eldest son would ask the Lord to bless the food, but his brother and father would jeer and ridicule him. When he asked them to be quiet while he said grace, the father angrily retorted, "Who do you think you are? Why must we be silent because of your stupid beliefs? Is your God deaf? Can't He hear what you are saying? He should listen more carefully."

This was persecution from his own family. He had to stand alone but, despite the insults, he remained faithful to Jesus and at church he found a brand-new family, "brothers" and "sisters" who surrounded him with love.

If we follow Jesus and obey Him, the world will hate us. Persecution and hate can be evaded by hiding the faith in

one's heart and living as in the world. Such faith, however, is dead, for we may not hide our faith. "Let your life
so shine before men ..." (Matthew 5:16), we are commanded.

A young man was called up for military service. On his
first vacation home the local minister called in at his
house. After the small talk was over, the clergyman
asked the soldier what reaction he noticed when witnessing his faith. Surprised, the soldier answered, "Why, no
reaction at all. They did not even notice I was a Christian." Our faith must be seen, our confession must be
heard and our life-style must endorse it.

## Thermometer or Thermostat Christians?

Many Christians are like thermometers. Their tem-
perature rises when it is warm and drops when it gets
cold. A meeting can often make some of them warm. They
sing, pray and look very spiritual until one day they get
into the company of non-Christians, and the mercury
quickly falls to the world's level. Thermometer Christians
adapt to the circumstances surrounding them.

Christians should be like thermostats. The thermostat
does not adapt to circumstances but regulates the tem-
perature. So should Christians regulate the spiritual tem-
perature around them. Their ability to do this will evoke
criticism or hatred, but such persecution is a sign of true
discipleship. "Blessed are you when men hate you ... and
revile you ... on account of the Son of man! Rejoice in
that day, and leap for joy ..." (Luke 6:22-23). Nowhere in
the Bible is persecution given as a sign of defeat. In fact,
being persecuted for one's faith is to be considered an
honor.

Thermometer Christians will never be persecuted.
They are Christians with fellow-believers, but when they
are among non-Christians they act as non-believers do.
They will not be reviled by the world, neither will they be
honored by God.

**When Persecution Comes**

What attitude should we adopt when persecuted? Here are some guidelines taken from the Bible:

1. *Fear not.* We need never fear, because God cares for us, especially in the day of trial and persecution.

2. Persecution is a mark of *true discipleship.* A Christian is never a victim of circumstances.

3. Persecution is *directed at Jesus* and not at the Christian. Saul persecuted the church, yet Jesus said, "Why do you persecute *me*?" (Acts 9:4).

4. *Rejoice* despite persecution. "Rejoice in so far as you share Christ's sufferings ... If one suffers as a Christian, let him not be ashamed, but under that name let him glorify God" (1 Peter 4:13, 16).

5. *Pray for boldness* in times of persecution. When the disciples were persecuted, they prayed for boldness to speak His word (Acts 4:24-30). It was a noteworthy prayer. It contained no disappointment, nor did it ask that persecution be removed. The disciples prayed for power, which they received, because they were filled with the Holy Spirit and spoke with boldness.

6. *Do not be surprised* when persecution comes. "A servant is not greater than his master. If they persecuted me, they will persecute you" (John 15:20). "Do not be surprised at the fiery ordeal ... as though something strange were happening to you" (1 Peter 4:12).

7. Persecution is a *privilege.* "Blessed are you when men revile you and persecute you . . . on my account" (Matthew 5:11). "Rejoice in that day, and leap for joy ..." (Luke 6:23). As strange as it may be, the reaction to persecution according to the Bible can only be, "Praise the Lord for persecution!"

Many people, when they suffer for their faith, say, "What does the Lord have against me? Why am I suffering in this way?" Instead, they should look upon it as a privilege, for the devil only attacks believers who are really alive.

George, a butler at a stately English home, was one of those people who was always bemoaning the fact that he was being tempted and persecuted by the devil. One day he confided in his master.

"Sir, I keep having these bad dreams that can only come from Satan himself," he said.

His employer laughed. "That's where I am lucky, George. I don't believe in God or Satan, so I never have a problem like that."

The conversation took place on a moor in a lonely part of northern England where the British lord had gone out for a grouse shoot. George's task was to carry the guns and look after the hunting dog.

He watched as his employer took aim and shot two birds in quick succession. One spiralled to the ground and lay dead a hundred yards away. The other game bird was hit but not fatally injured. It desperately flapped its wings trying to keep airborne. Slowly it lost height and finally fell to the ground, but was still alive.

"Quick, Rover, get the grouse," the master ordered the dog, which bounded enthusiastically towards the dead bird. Within a minute, tail wagging proudly, the dog came back with the lifeless bird in its mouth.

"No, you stupid dog, not the dead one! I wanted you to go and finish off the one that was still alive."

George looked at his master and said, "Now I know why the Devil wants me and not you."

You see, when we are spiritually dead, we pose no problem for Satan. It's when we are alive and active that we cause him so many headaches. So he attacks in every way possible.

Rather than being upset with this, however, we should realize that this is a mark of a true Christian, a real disciple.

Chapter 2

## POINTS FOR PERSONAL REFLECTION

1. What are the basic reasons for the testings and persecution that Christians suffer? (John 15:18-21; Acts 9:4, 5)

2. Why do many Christians eventually forsake Christ? (Matthew 13:18-23)

3. What should our attitude be towards those who persecute us? (Matthew 5:44; Luke 23:24)

4. What was the content of the disciples' prayer when they were persecuted? (Acts 4:27-31)

5. Describe both the suffering and the victory described in Romans 8:31-39. How does this apply to us?

# Chapter 3

# THE HOLY SPIRIT AND PERSECUTION

The Holy Spirit is the source of power of every Christian. This is particularly so in times of persecution, when unity and courage are vital. The apostles experienced this. Before Pentecost the disciples were afraid of the Jews. After Pentecost the Jews were afraid of the disciples. After they had been filled with the Holy Spirit at Pentecost, the disciples were changed from being fearful to being full of courage.

Before Pentecost, a maid identified Peter as being one of the disciples. Fear made him deny his Master. Despite his best intentions, he was unable to make good his boast. Before Jesus' arrest Peter vehemently denied that he would ever renounce his Master and added that he was willing to die for Him. A few hours later, however, he denied Jesus three times, because he was afraid that his life might be required of him. The price of discipleship turned out to be too high: "I do not know Him" was his response.

After Pentecost he was again recognized: "Now when they saw the boldness of Peter and John . . . they wondered; and they recognized that they had been with Jesus" (Acts 4:13). Peter did not hesitate but spoke with authority and power. "But you shall receive power when the Holy Spirit has come upon you . . ." (Acts 1:8).

Peter and the other disciples were true followers of Jesus. They loved Him. They had sacrificed much. Yet before Pentecost their eyes were still closed to the greatest sacrifice of all. The "I" was still on the throne instead of the Lord. While Jesus was preparing for His suffering and death, the disciples were contending with one another on who would be the greatest (Luke 9:46).

These types of disciples are still in existence. Despite

their pious ways, they live not to glorify Christ but to glorify themselves and to satisfy their own egos. They have to be top dog at their church or in their ministry. Whoever dares to differ with them is the object of their derision and scorn.

One cold winter's night, the German pessimistic philosopher, Arthur Schopenhauer, happened to see two porcupines. They shivered with cold. They crept towards each other in an attempt to gain some warmth. As soon as the spiky creatures touched, their quills jabbed into one another and inflicted pain. Thus they would shrink back, only to try again later. Schopenhauer made the observation that many Christians behave in the same manner. Though they know the need for one another, as soon as they get too close they hurt each other.

God does not want Christians to live on their own. He wants us to have fellowship without hurting one another. The Holy Spirit is the one who makes this possible: "For by one Spirit we were all baptized into one body — Jews or Greeks, slaves or free — and all were made to drink of one Spirit" (1 Corinthians 12:13).

We are able, through the Holy Spirit, to live together and glorify God. Unity can be experienced only through the Holy Spirit, whether you are Chinese, Negro, Indian or Caucasian. The basis of fellowship is not creed or color, culture or position, but new life in Christ Jesus. Without the Holy Spirit you will inflict pain.

The night Jesus was betrayed, the disciples still refused to wash one another's feet. Each one wanted to be the most important, and did not understand that he, who was willing to be the least, would become the greatest. In the end Jesus Himself became the servant.

Just a few days before, the Apostle John turned out to be a sectarian: "Master, we saw a man casting out demons in your name, and we forbade him, because he does not follow with *us*" (Luke 9:49). In all honesty I must add that the disciples, though denominationalists, did not behave quite as badly as some modern-day believers. They at least cast out demons. Many Christians today are unable to do this and will sharply criticize those who are in earnest about this instruction. The disciples fortunately acknowledged the reality of the powers of darkness. Their objection was that another brother had performed the miracle, someone who did not belong to their denomination.

"Someone who does not follow with *us*," is the motto of sectarianism, against which He (the Holy Spirit) is the only remedy. For when the Holy Spirit takes control, then our concern expands. It is no longer for "*our* church and tradition" but for the glory and honor of Christ Jesus. To glorify Jesus is the purpose of the Holy Spirit in each child of God. To be fully surrendered to the Holy Spirit is the path of steadfastness in times of persecution.

Every child of God has received the Holy Spirit (Ephesians 1:13). This does not mean that we are always automatically surrendered to the Spirit. Many people live off an experience of the Holy Spirit that occurred many years previously. When they give their testimonies, they talk about the great happening in their lives when they were flooded with the power of the Spirit. But what of now?

We must be more concerned with what the Holy Spirit is doing in our lives *today* than in what happened years ago. We are to be continuously filled by the Holy Spirit, but sometimes obstructions occur.

## Clear the Obstruction

One day while still in Laos I went to a little village in the mountains, just north of the royal capital at Luang Prabang.

Despite the fact that they have no irrigation, the villagers had designed a unique system. The town was situated in a valley and farther up on a hill was a spring. No one knew where the water came from, and because it came out of the mountain they called it the "mountain spring." This spring developed into a rivulet which passed through the valley.

However, the people did not use river water for drinking purposes. They had another method to get drinking water. At the spring, water was caught in a large basin and, from there, it flowed into a bamboo pipe to the village below. The top part was left open in case twigs blocked the flow of the water. In this way it would be easy to check where the obstruction was.

When I visited the village the water had stopped flowing, although the river was still quite full. "Nothing serious," the village headman told me. "The river is full of water, so the pipe must be blocked."

I accompanied him as he walked up along the bamboo conduit. It did not take long to discover that twigs had in fact collected in the pipe, and leaves had been sucked up against the twigs. The blockage caused the water to flow over the sides of the pipe.

To me this is a beautiful example of the working of the Holy Spirit. At times He is unable to flow freely through our lives. He is there, but there is an obstruction. We have to return to the place where sin has blocked the stream; the obstruction must be removed before the Holy Spirit can work unhindered.

When Christians ask how to live in the Holy Spirit, the answer is simple: Remove the wrong in your life, empty yourself and make way for the Spirit. Confess your sins to the Lord. If you empty yourself, then the Holy Spirit can fill you with His power and presence.

Christians who have experienced persecution testify to the necessity of being filled with the Holy Spirit. Laotian church leader Brother Soeban was interned in a Communist brainwashing camp on three different occasions. They tried to break his spirit by indoctrinating him with atheistic propaganda for weeks at a time.

"At times it seemed almost too much for me," Soeban, once a former Captain in the Royal Laotian army, told me. "That I could remain steadfast was only possible because of the indwelling of the Holy Spirit. When things became too rough, I would often hear the voice of the Holy Spirit. He would encourage me and point me to Jesus, who had suffered more than I. He assured me that He would keep me from falling. This gave me power and joy. I knew I was not alone. The Comforter was always with me."

Soeban heard that still small voice of the Holy Spirit in a concentration camp because he learned to listen to His voice while he was still a free man. If we surrender ourselves to the Holy Spirit and learn to walk in His power while we still live in freedom, then the Holy Spirit will guide us now and also in the future.

Soeban was a fiery evangelist. I had the privilege of working with him for a few years. In fact we both lived in the same town. Wherever he went, he witnessed and he led many Laotians to Jesus. Because he used his freedom to work for the Lord, he was able to continue to witness in the concentration camp. Whoever is ashamed of Christ now will be even more ashamed of Him during persecution. Those who live for Him now will continue to live for Him when scorned and persecuted.

Soeban also witnessed to his Communist guards. One of them accepted the Lord Jesus. A miracle happened the next day. The Communist leaders came to the conclusion that they would not be able to break Soeban's spirit, despite their indoctrination and torture. Soeban had survived three terms in concentration camp and still witnessed for Christ. The leaders then decided that they would have to kill him.

In the room where this decision took place there were only the Communist officers. At the door was a guard. He overheard the conversation. This soldier was the same man Soeban had led to the Lord the day before. The Lord had arranged for this man to be on guard that morning, and on hearing the decision he was much afraid but said nothing. Then the Holy Spirit said to him: "I saved you through Soeban yesterday. Now I want to save Soeban through you." That night the guard helped Soeban escape.

The Holy Spirit is the Comforter in times of persecution. He does not keep us trouble-free but imparts power so that, in spite of trials, we can remain faithful.

The Lord permits us to go through persecution because He knows that Christ's love and the power of the Holy Spirit will enable us to be more than conquerors. But whoever does not live in the Holy Spirit during freedom will have difficulty remaining faithful in times of persecution. The price of discipleship will be too high.

Three men walking down a street stopped outside a beautiful house and began arguing about who really owned the property.

The first said, "That is my house because I built it."

"No, you're wrong," protested the second. "I bought it. It's mine."

The third smiled and added, "Yes. But I now live in it."

That is a beautiful illustration of the life of a Christian. God built us; His son Jesus Christ bought us on the cross; and now the Holy Spirit lives in us.

When we are truly surrendered to the Holy Spirit, we have a new boldness that nothing can quench. I remember a visit to Uganda with Brother Andrew at the time when Idi Amin was still terrorizing the country with his satanic excesses.

A woman believer had come to see us at the Kampala International Hotel, which at that time was infested with Amin's so-called secret police. (Actually they were easily identified because most of them wore flowered shirts, dark glasses, bell-bottom trousers and platform-heel shoes.)

As we all stepped into the elevator I noticed that we were joined by one of these policemen, who was taking a great interest in us. He obviously wanted to know what a Ugandan woman was doing with two foreigners. I felt my heart flutter a little, knowing that there was the possibility that one or all of us could be hauled off to prison.

Suddenly the woman believer smiled at the policeman, opened her purse, took out a tract and handed it to him.

"Brother, please take this. Jesus loves you and wants to save you," she said softly. He was startled, but as her smile burst into an all-consuming grin, he took it. With a flustered look, he stuffed it into his pocket.

She had a boldness that could only have come from the Holy Spirit. Do you have that same boldness? You can have it, if you allow God's Spirit to fill you.

Chapter 3

## POINTS FOR PERSONAL REFLECTION

1. Why did God send the Holy Spirit? Read John 14:16-17, 26; John 16:8, 14; Romans 8:16.

2. Do the fruits of the Spirit described in Galatians 5:22-23 have any application in times of persecution?

3. The gifts of the Spirit are listed in Romans 12:6-8 and I Corinthians 12:7-11. Who receives these gifts? How are they to be used? How will the distribution of these gifts be useful to us in times of persecution, when churches may not be able to function?

# Chapter 4

# THE BIBLE AND THE SUFFERING CHURCH

During the Vietnam war, a number of American soldiers were captured and taken to the north's capital, Hanoi. After they had been kept under strict surveillance for a few weeks, they decided to read from the Bible to one another. They asked one of the guards for a Bible, but the man just shook his head.

They then decided to write a Bible for themselves, from memory. Each soldier quoted verses he knew from the Bible.

It started off with a flourish. One after another they quoted Bible verses, as one POW acted as secretary, writing all the verses on a piece of paper.

Too soon they realized how limited their Bible knowledge was. Except for John 3:16, Psalm 23, the "Our Father" and the Ten Commandments, they could remember only a few more verses. They stared at one another dejectedly; in an hour they had perhaps twenty verses. They kept on trying, only to discover that they were confusing one verse with another.

It was obvious. The Word of God did not dwell in them richly. No matter how hard they tried, they could not quote any more verses correctly. "Let the word of Christ dwell in you richly . . ." (Colossians 3:16).

## A Banned Book

The Bible is a banned book in times of persecution. In China, Laos and Vietnam, the Communists either burned or confiscated thousands of Bibles. When the Christians assembled, they could do little more than the American prisoners of war. They tried to quote the Bible but did not get very far. The reason was simple. While they lived in freedom they had not seen the need for Bible memorization. Why exert yourself by learning Bible texts if you have a Bible on your bookshelf?

The general opinion was that the revolution would not take place. When it *did* take place, the Church obviously was not prepared. When the Christians saw the necessity of Bible memorization, it was too late. One cannot attempt to learn Bible verses once the Bibles have been confiscated or burned. It takes time and it must start while there is still freedom.

In many Communist countries the Bible is now a banned book. The only way to get the Word of God to Christians is to smuggle it in, although many Communist governments import a limited number of Bibles. But the amount is so small that only a few congregations receive the benefit. Such official importation is done to create for the outside world the impression of religious freedom.

To the Communists, the Bible remains a dangerous book. If Bibles are sold, conditions are usually attached. One is that any Christian wishing to buy a Bible must join a registered church, and his purchase is listed with the government. In this way the Communists can keep track of who the Christians are.

## The Suffering Church

Atheistic governments recognize that Christianity can never be completely eradicated. Therefore they attempt to restrict religious freedom in a number of ways:

1. The churches and their members must be registered. This becomes a means for the state to control church functions and to have access to the membership rolls.

2. Christians are permitted to worship and to talk about the Lord only inside the registered church building. Public evangelism is prohibited in most Communist countries.

3. Christians are forbidden to teach religion to children; therefore Sunday schools and youth gatherings are not allowed. Even within the home, Christian training is not to take place.

4. Christians are given the less desirable menial jobs: their children are not allowed a university education. They are, in effect, second class citizens.

Many Christians have accepted these conditions, and tried to work within the limitations imposed. Other Christians, however, have refused to register, because they believe this would be compromise with an atheistic government. They would rather obey God than the Communist leaders. They believe they should continue to evangelize openly. It is dangerous, but they form "secret" churches and continue with Sunday schools and youth meetings.

It is this latter group which is persecuted, in Russia, in China, and elsewhere. These Christians suffer because of the name of Jesus. If they evangelize, they can be arrested, but they are willing to pay a price for their faith. Many of them have suffered in prison as a result.

Aida Skripnakova's testimony is well-known in the West. This Russian Christian from Leningrad would not stop evangelizing. She wrote her own tracts and handed them out in the streets of that historic city. She was arrested many times. Finally she was faced with a decision: to go to prison or to stop evangelizing. She chose to surrender her freedom rather than be disobedient to Jesus, because her loyalty to Jesus meant more to her than freedom.

From prison Aida penned a letter; it was smuggled out and reached us in the West a few weeks later. Its contents moved our hearts, because it witnessed to her consecration to the Lord. She wrote, "The authorities offered me freedom on the condition that I keep quiet about Jesus. I cannot do it. I cannot compromise. Such freedom would then become my greatest bondage."

What courage and dedication! She would rather remain behind bars than stop witnessing. She was prepared to pay the high price of discipleship.

There are hundreds of thousands of Christians who would rather suffer than compromise with an atheistic government. They make up what we now call the Suffering Church. In the Book of Revelation, such believers are described as "overcomers."

Fifteen pastors in Mozambique decided recently to

hold a baptism service for believers who wanted to testify publicly to what had happened to them. But to hold such a ceremony they had to seek permission from the Marxist Frelimo government.

They met to pray and discuss what they should do and they agreed that the Scriptures taught that they should honor their government. So they asked for official permission, but it was refused.

"If you hold a baptism service, we will arrest all of your pastors," they were told by an irate Frelimo official.

What should they do? The leaders knew that the Bible also taught that they should *obey God* rather than men.

"Right, we will hold the service and we will do it in the open air. Whatever the consequences, we will not hide away in secret," their leaders decided.

So on the banks of one of Mozambique's rivers, they held a highly dangerous baptismal service. There the believers showed they were willing to "die with Christ" as the baptism signified.

As the service was ending, soldiers pounced and, at rifle point, hauled all the pastors off to prison. Yet they counted it a joy to suffer for Christ.

Finally, after three months they were freed. Through the power of the Holy Spirit, however, they had become overcomers.

## Is It Necessary to Smuggle Bibles?

Open Doors is now engaged in Project Pearl, an audacious plan to take one million Bibles into the People's Republic of China — the largest operation of its kind undertaken by our organization.

The million Bibles are being taken in through the Bamboo Curtain at the request of China's secret believers with whom Open Doors has forged contacts over the past few years.

But why take in Bibles in clandestine ways such as this? The so-called smugglers come in for quite a hammering from some parts of the Christian Church. After all, aren't the Chinese printing their own Bibles?

The printing they refer to is of a promised 100,000 New

Testaments. Controversy has surrounded this possibility because the translation that would be used is one being re-done within China, with variations included to incorporate changes in expression found in modern Chinese.

"You see," said one Chinese leader, "even if they go ahead with this printing, the changes they put into the words of the Scriptures might water down the true message. We could not use such a Bible."

He also voiced a second major fear. "We are wondering whether we will ever see these Bibles that the government is promising. Our guess is that they will be placed in libraries and places of learning where we cannot easily have access to them." This has been the pattern among many Communist countries of the world who are allowing some Bibles to be imported or printed.

Open Doors alone took into China more than 30,000 Bibles in 1979 — almost one third of the total the government promised it would print. Our leader had already heard of the massive need for Scriptures inside China, and knew for a fact that the need was well into the millions. How far would 100,000 go?

Brother Andrew has focused on this same point. "The problem between official and unofficial distribution," he said, "is that usually, no matter how many copies a Communist government is prepared to print or import, you can be sure that in every case the supply is a long way short of the demand. Maybe a trickle of Scriptures will be supplied to a population, but they still desperately need more to be supplied unofficially. We should not disappoint them."

I knew many Christians were skeptical about Bible "smuggling," so I decided during one of my trips to Eastern Europe to investigate at first hand the answers to two questions:

1. Was it really necessary to smuggle Bibles?

2. Was it wise to distribute these Scriptures free of charge? Would it not be better to ask the recipients to pay a small fee? Would the Bibles then not have more value to them?

Now, after many years, I feel ashamed for ever having asked the second question. How can one expect these believers to pay for a Bible we can afford to give them when they have already paid the highest price of all? Members of the Suffering Church will not compromise with the authorities; they are prepared to be persecuted; they prefer prison to disobeying Christ. They cannot obtain a Bible unless we take it to them. Dare we still ask if it is appreciated if we give it to them free?

I should like to elaborate on the first question, however. I do not like the term smuggling; it reminds me of the type of people who smuggle diamonds, watches, and even drugs, to be resold at a profit. The possibility of their illicit gain is, in fact, an integral part of the definition of smuggling.

We, however, do not have that motivation. We *buy* Bibles, carry them in and distribute them free of charge. To those who still find it difficult to accept this type of ministry, I would like to suggest a book written by Brother Andrew, *Why I Smuggle Bibles* (previously titled, *The Ethics of Smuggling*), an exceptional work containing a tremendous challenge. It may be obtained at the address which appears at the end of this book.

Because I had heard so often that it really was not necessary to smuggle Bibles, as Bibles were being imported via official channels, I made an investigation into this on one of my trips to Eastern Europe. I met a leader of one of the unregistered churches who told me his congregation needed Bibles urgently.

"But one can buy these Bibles in the city," I said.

"I know," he answered, "but *we* cannot buy the Bibles, because we are not registered."

"Let's go see," I suggested.

He looked at me doubtfully. "It can be dangerous for my congregation," he argued.

He was right. I could not endanger his congregation unnecessarily. I decided to forget it.

But then the minister continued, "All right, I'll go, so you can see for yourself."

I hesitated, feeling guilty because I knew I could expose him to danger.

"Anyway, they don't know me," he added. "But we must be careful not to be seen together. After we visit the bookshop, we must leave in different directions to make sure we are not followed."

We decided to enter the shop shortly after one another, acting as though we did not know each other. I would purchase a Bible and then he would do so afterwards. This we did. I entered the shop, and the minister followed soon afterward.

The man behind the counter looked up amiably and asked if he could help me. I asked if he spoke English or German. Yes, he could understand German, he answered in a friendly manner.

"I want to buy a Bible," I said.

"Are you a tourist?" he asked in broken German.

"Yes, from Holland," I replied.

This appeared to be sufficient, because he disappeared into a backroom and returned a moment later with a stack of Bibles. He displayed them on the counter and said I could choose one. The prices seemed reasonable.

I paid for one copy and asked if I could browse around for a while in the bookshop. I wanted to see what would transpire.

Eventually it was the pastor's turn to be served. I could not understand every word exchanged, because they spoke in their own language, but what I could make out was sufficient. (Later my friend related the whole account to me, although it was no longer necessary, for what had happened was clear enough.)

The pastor pointed to the Bibles and asked to buy one. A long discourse ensued.

"Who are you, and with which church are you registered?" the shopkeeper asked.

The pastor shook his head. He just wanted to buy one Bible without having to disclose all the information. The shopkeeper remained friendly and almost appeared apologetic. He would like to be of service but had to keep to the regulations. This necessitated his knowing which church the man had joined.

Finally the salesman took the Bibles back into the storeroom. My friend left without me. I had seen enough, but I remained a while longer to ward off suspicion.

Although I was happy to be able to give the Bible I had

bought to the minister, I had received clear proof of the need of the Suffering Church.

Don't misunderstand me — we are grateful for the Bibles which the Bible societies may take in legally, and the situation has greatly improved in recent years in some countries, though not having kept pace with the population growth or with the increasing number of Christians. Yet both official and unregistered churches need the Word of God. In rural areas especially, few couriers ever reach the many congregations without Scripture. Orthodox and Catholic churches in the Soviet Union are as needy as any of the unregistered evangelical grups. It is for all these we willingly continue with the often dangerous work of taking in Bibles in unauthorized ways.

## The Following Page

It is important to know the situation of the Suffering Church, because it helps us understand the need for Bible memorization. I had the opportunity to address a secret gathering of believers in remote Siberia some time ago. I read to them a portion of Scripture out of an English Bible. Besides the leader and myself, only a few others had a copy of the Scriptures. I was dumbstruck and could only look at the few who possessed Bibles with tears in my eyes. Those who had them held God's Word at such an angle that the people sitting next to and behind them could also see and read. Many stretched their necks in order to read a few words.

Back in my hotel, I thought of an occurrence which took place in this little town in Siberia not so long ago. One of our Open Doors couriers had visited this particular area and had met a Christian who showed him a leaf taken from the Bible.

"Look, I also have a page from the Bible," the man beamed.

"Why do you have only one page?" the courier asked.

"Oh, I got it from someone," the brother answered. "A while back someone gave our leader a Bible. He already had one, so he decided to give it away. The question was:

To whom? There were so many Christians without Bibles. Finally, to satisfy everyone, he divided the Bibles among the Christians. He split it up into sections and gave each Christian a book of the Bible."

The courier stared at him in amazement. "But why do you then have only one page?"

"Unfortunately, I wasn't there when this happened," he recounted. "I met one of the brothers who had received a share, and he gave a page each to a few Christians, including me."

They talked a little while longer. The Siberian Christian asked the courier for a Bible, but he explained sadly that he had given them all away in the previous town. The believer gave a sigh and said wistfully, "I would have liked to know what was on the next page."

## Lack of Knowledge

We have the next pages and know the contents — or do we? The prisoners of war in Vietnam thought they knew, but they did not. When the Bible was no longer available, they tried to recall the Word of God, but it was evident that their knowledge was limited.

Bible memorization cannot be started the moment the Bible is scarce. It must begin while there is still religious freedom and the Bible is freely available. It takes time and effort.

For us, however, the obstacle is not the effort but the thought that persecution will not come. It came to Russia, China and Vietnam. The Bible became a banned book. Many Christians there do not even possess a Bible, let alone being able to memorize it. They had never seen the necessity of Bible memorization during the time of religious freedom. Even though the revolution had begun, they still believed that the Bible would always be available. This was a false hope. Bibles were impounded and burned. It was too late to start Bible memorization. Now most Christians don't know what the next page holds.

Hosea 4:6 gives a clear warning: "My people are destroyed for lack of knowledge." Yes, there is lack of knowledge. If we would have greater insight into the revolution which has swept the world, we undoubtedly would give more time to commit the Bible to memory.

While it is imperative that we send Bibles to the Suffering Church, we also must use the opportunity to memorize God's Word. Soon we will realize that Bible knowledge is useful, not only for the future but also for the present. Because we are continuously fighting sin and the powers of darkness, *now* is the time to know and use God's Word!

"Thy word is a lamp to my feet and a light to my path" (Psalm 119:105).

This implies that our path is dark and dangerous.

"I have laid up thy word in my heart, that I might not sin against thee" (Psalm 119:11).

God's Word must be kept in our hearts instead of on the bookshelf. Then we will know from experience that the Word of God is the sword of the Spirit (Ephesians 6:17). Jesus knew this. When the devil tested Him in the desert, He used the Scriptures. Every time the devil tempted Him, Jesus answered, "It is written. . . ." He quoted the Word of God.

The devil's tactics have not changed. He knows the Bible, but when he quotes it, he takes it out of context (Matthew 4:6). We should not be ignorant of his designs (2 Corinthians 2:11). He will tell us that it is not necessary to memorize the Bible, that it is enough to have it in the house, in case it is needed. God's Word tells us differently. It reminds us to let it dwell in us richly (Colossians 3:16), to enable us to manage the spiritual battle now and in the future.

Many good methods exist for Bible memorization. An international organization, The Navigators, gives excellent memorization courses. The texts are carefully chosen and cover various subjects, e.g., Christ the Head, obedience, prayer, witnessing, sin, deliverance, assurance, the Holy Spirit, worldliness, steadfastness, evangelism, purity, faith and many other subjects.

By memorizing the Word daily, our characters are developed and our spirits are nourished. It has an influence on our reactions and decisions, and the Holy Spirit will bring the Word to our remembrance when needed. Dawson Trotman, the founder of The Navigators, once said, "Nothing yields as much fruit as time devoted to writing God's Word on the tablets of your heart." Bible memorization enables us to apply God's will in our daily lives. It is a weapon against worldliness and a means to arrive at Christlikeness.

One Christian leader has said, "The Bible keeps us from sin, but sin keeps us from Bible memorization." If we take time filling our minds and thoughts with the Word of God, the Holy Spirit will be able to renew us from within. "He who does not love me does not keep my words . . ." (John 14:24). The opposite is also true: "If a man loves me, he will keep my word, and my Father will love him, and we will come to him and make our home with him" (John 14:23).

## Practical Methods for Bible Memorization

1. First of all you need a few cards on which Bible verses can be written. Write the verse on one side and the reference on the other.

2. Read the verse aloud, and then repeat the words without looking at the card. Then read the Bible reference on the other side and repeat the Bible verse again.

3. Try to learn a verse a day, but don't learn the next verse until you know the first.

4. Repeat the Bible verses you learned the previous day.

5. Always keep the cards with you. With a little effort and willpower you will always find a quiet moment to repeat the verses and learn a new one.

Regularity and perseverance are needed. The devil won't like your decision to memorize God's Word. He will discourage you when learning new verses or repeating the previous ones. Trust in the Lord and His promise: "I can do all things in him who strengthens me" (Philippians 4:13).

Remember, the key to success is not only God's promise but also your perseverance. Repeat, repeat, repeat. "If you abide in me, and my words abide in you, ask whatever you will, and it shall be done for you" (John 15:7).

Our eldest son attends a school where Bible memorization is an essential part of their religious instruction. We are happy about this. I did not know, however, the kind of Bible verses he had to learn until one day he came to me and said, "Daddy, please check to see if I know my Bible verses."

He didn't sound too enthusiastic. When I read the verses I realized why. These were the verses he had to recite the next day:

Judges 4:14: "And Deborah said to Barak, 'Up! For this is the day in which the Lord has given Sisera into your hand. Does not the Lord go out before you?' So Barak went down from Mount Tabor with ten thousand men following him."

Second Samuel 1:25, 26: "How are the mighty fallen in the midst of battle! Jonathan lies down upon thy high places. I am distressed for you, my brother Jonathan; very pleasant have you been to me; your love to me was wonderful, passing the love of women."

Luke 20:18: "Every one who falls on that stone will be broken to pieces; but when it falls on anyone it will crush him."

He still had to learn several more. No wonder he sounded so discouraged! Such Bible verses indeed crush those who have to learn them. It does not foster love for Bible memorization, but only aversion.

Before choosing any verses, we would advise you to follow a course such as that of The Navigators. Discuss this with the members of your church or Bible study group. If you think you do not need such a course, I would advise you after reading this chapter to take pen and paper and give yourself a Bible knowledge test. Write down all Bible verses and references you know on a piece of paper. The captured American soldiers did not get very far. How far will you get?

Chapter 4

## POINTS FOR PERSONAL REFLECTION

1. Spiritual immaturity and a lack of Bible knowledge often go hand in hand. Read Hebrews 4:12-16 and consider the active role the Word of God plays in our relationship to God's grace and mercy.

2. Read through Psalm 119, marking the specific references to the Word of God. Examine each truth, to see if it is as applicable to us as it was to the psalmist.

3. The activity of the Holy Spirit in inspiring Scripture is closely linked to the role He has in our life and walk with the Lord. How is this a part of Jesus' concern for us? (John 16:12-15)

## Chapter 5

# CHILD EVANGELIZING

After an evangelistic meeting in the United States, a man approached Dwight L. Moody, the well-known American preacher, and asked him if anyone had been converted that night. Moody smiled and answered, "Yes, two-and-a-half were saved."

The man looked puzzled. Then, as if the light had dawned, he said, "You mean two adults and a child?"

"No," Moody corrected him, "I mean two children and one adult."

This puzzled the man even more, so the evangelist went on to explain, "Children have their lives ahead of them, while adults are already past the halfway mark."

Moody was right. Children do have their lives ahead of them. The Communists know this too. Their motto is, "Give us children until they are twelve, then you may have them." During those twelve years the children can be fully indoctrinated with atheistic propaganda. Children are more receptive during these years. That is when their characters are formed. This is the reason Sunday schools are forbidden. Great efforts are taken to bring the children up in an atheistic way of thought.

Indoctrination starts very early. Not only do the men work, but the women too. Children are sent to state-run day-care centers and are reared in a godless climate. The state is aware of the mother's influence on a child, so it compels her to work all day. Back at home in the evening, she is too tired to devote much time and attention to the child.

It is my opinion that we, who live in a materialistic world, follow the same tactic as the Communists. The number of working women has increased drastically over the past few years. We need to examine this trend carefully in order to find the correct balance. Our children should not be left to their own devices.

According to Deuteronomy 6:5 we must love God with our whole heart, soul and might, and the seventh verse says, "You shall teach them (the words of this commandment) diligently to your children, and shall talk of them when you sit in your house, and when you walk by the way, and when you lie down, and when you rise."

To sum up, one can say that we need to give much time and attention to our children. To prevent parents from giving needed love and teaching to their children, Communist governments compel women to work all day; and in the western world Mammon (the money god) keeps mothers out of the homes. In both cases the children suffer as a result.

### Who Makes the Decision — the Children?

Sometime ago I had a talk with a young couple. They had two children, and we discussed the importance of a Christian upbringing. The husband totally disagreed with my view that the children should be reared "in the fear of the Lord."

"There is no question about it," he said. "I will allow my children to make their own decisions. As far as I'm concerned, they don't have to say grace, they don't need to attend a Christian school, nor do they have to attend church or Sunday school. This way they will develop freely and independently. When they are bigger, they can decide what they want to do. I don't want to force them to go. They can choose for themselves at a later stage."

He seemed to forget that his children live in a world which is sinful. While keeping them back from places where the Gospel is preached, he exposes them to the influences of the world. You cannot allow your children to grow up neutral, because there is no such position. That is why the Communists say, "Give us the children until they are twelve."

That is also why Jesus said, "Let the children come to me" (Matthew 19:14); "Train up a child in the way he should go, and when he is old he will not depart from it" (Proverbs 22:6); and, "Remember also your Creator in the days of your youth . . ." (Ecclesiastes 12:1).

God's existence is denied in Communist countries. Man is god in their view. The Communists train the children according to their way, convinced that they will not depart from it.

A teacher in a Russian school once told her pupils that there was no God. "God does not exist," she said. "The Christians in our country pray to their God, but how can He help them if He does not exist?"

She ordered a boy, whom she knew had Christian parents, to stand up. "Look, he is a Christian," she said. "Do you also pray to God?" she asked the boy.

The poor little fellow nodded timidly.

"Good," she continued. "You may sit down, close your eyes and ask God if He won't put a candy on your desk."

The boy wanted to say something, but dared not reply.

"Never mind," the teacher insisted. "Just pray to your God and see what happens."

The child could only obey, so he closed his eyes. While the other children looked on, the teacher placed the goodie on his desk.

"Now, open your eyes quickly and see what your God has done!" she said.

The boy stared at the candy on his desk in amazement. Was it a miracle? The whole class chortled, especially when the teacher said, "You most probably thought your God put it there? Forget it, dear boy. I put it there."

In this way and many others, faith is ridiculed. Children from Christian homes are considered heroes if they inform teachers exactly what their parents believe and where they meet on Sunday. And children do betray their parents — as a consequence of constant atheistic propaganda.

Lenin once said. "We must hate. Hatred is the basis of Communism. Children must be taught to hate their parents if they are Christians."

Because children are guileless, the Communists use them to find out where Christians come together for their secret meetings. The police have often raided homes where such meetings were taking place, after the teachers got the information from the children at school and subsequently reported it to the authorities.

A statue has even been erected in honor of a Russian child who informed the K.G.B. on his Christian parents.

At a congress in Moscow, a former Russian commissioner of education Anatole Lunarcharsky, remonstrated against Christians in that country. He repeated Lenin's words — that hate is the basis of communism — and added, "We hate the Christians. They are a stumbling block in the development of the revolution. They preach forgiveness and love of one's neighbor, but that is the opposite of our principles. Away with neighborly love! We need hate! Only then can we conquer the world."

## The Testament of Her Older Brother

In spite of such propaganda, the Church of Jesus Christ continues to grow, even in Communist countries. Although the governments profess that only the older generation still believes in God, a large percentage of the Christians are under the age of twenty. I attended gatherings in Russia and Siberia where fifty percent of the Christians present were young people. The young people also have their own youth meetings. Sometimes they meet in homes, on other occasions in the forest. They have learned to evade the police.

One evening, a young lady was on her way to a youth meeting when police agents intercepted her. They had probably been watching her for some time without finding anything of which to accuse her. That evening they stopped the believer and asked where she was going.

She did not want to betray her fellow Christians, nor did she want to tell a lie. With a sorrowful look, she told the agents, "My eldest brother died, and we are gathering together as a family to read his testament."

The police believed her. They felt sorry for her and allowed her to go. That evening she did indeed read the testament of her eldest brother — Jesus! She told the truth. She only omitted to tell them that not only had her eldest brother died, but he also rose again. If she had, the agents would have sent her to a psychiatrist.

"With the youth, then you have the future," the saying goes. If the future does not appear too bright, then we ought to give more attention to the youth. Sunday school work, youth work and Christian teaching are of the greatest importance.

The task and calling of a teacher is important. The children are daily in their care. We as Christians ought to give the same time and attention to our children as the Communists give to theirs.

Liberalism and humanism have pervaded our school systems. Many youth workers and even some Sunday school teachers don't even know Jesus as their Lord and Savior.

Much youth work is done only to keep the children off the streets. That is not enough. Children should not only be entertained; they must be renewed. They need Jesus. We must present the message of the Gospel to each child now, so that "when he is old he will not depart from it."

We should allocate time to children during church services. It is important to take our youngsters to church, yes, but then they must also be involved. It happens often that the hymns which are sung and the sermons that are preached are not understood by the children. Consequently the service is not a pleasure but a boring duty, and we lose more than we gain. We need to involve them in the services and talk directly to them.

An arrangement could be made that children attend only a portion of the service, preferably the first part. We could sing hymns they know, or let them sing one alone. Parents would always appreciate this. Before the sermon commences, the children can go to their own meeting. Then they will hear a message which they can understand. This is far better than listening to a sermon which they cannot understand because it is intended for their parents. If the adults have difficulty in following the sermon, how much more the children!

The preacher and Sunday school teacher could get together and use the same theme. This will also create a better bond between the minister and the helpers. Some people feel it is not necessary to have the children leave halfway through the service, because they attend Sunday school afterwards. Poor children. Their parents can hardly sit still if the service lasts five minutes longer than usual, but the children have to listen to a sermon not meant for them, plus spend another hour at Sunday school.

Should children attend the service? Certainly, but give them attention. With a little effort much can be accomplished, if we want to.

Working with children should not be considered "extra" work. It must be an essential part of the local Christian community. "They have a life ahead of them," Moody aptly said. We have to give more attention to child evangelism, especially as the future appers so bleak.

Why do I emphasize this matter? In countries where communism has taken over, many young Christians have denied the Lord. Most affected were those young people who in times of freedom were not involved in the church service. To them, attending church services had been a formality and a duty. They did not really feel they were included, because the sermons were directed at the adults and not at them. They actually regarded the revolution as a welcome release. The congregations that involved the children had fewer problems with young people when communism stepped in.

Interestingly, evangelical churches in countries that lack religious freedom are showing us how to truly involve children and young people in worship. In the Soviet Union, for instance, congregations are not allowed to carry out individual children's work and so compensate by other means. Choirs and orchestras are formed and rehearsal becomes the chief mode of fellowship together.

In other countries of East Europe, youth work is more tolerated. Children participate in services in Romania, for example, reading poetry and singing duets or reciting Scripture. Youth camps and other types of special youth activities in East Germany, Poland and Hungary are means by which the church nurtures its young.

It is possible to bring them into the worship life of the church. Many young people are grateful for this experience because much of what they memorized for the services as children, they have never forgotten.

The Communists realize that the battle for the minds of

children is equally as important as the battles fought with guns and missiles.

This was forcefully brought home to me during a visit to the once proud land of Ethiopia, which until a few years ago had been a unique Coptic Christian state, isolated from 300 AD. The revolution came there in 1974 after army officers deposed Emperor Haile Selassie. The army officers ruled through a committee called the Dergue, which announced in 1975 that it would pursue socialist (Marxist) policies.

I discovered that, over a three-year period, the Communists there had imported two million books on Marxism and published internally more than eight million pieces of literature on atheistic beliefs. Almost all of this propaganda was aimed at young people.

"Brother Jan," one Christian leader told me sadly, "the Communists have spent more than 50 percent of their time and effort since taking over the country in indoctrinating the children."

Often their methods are extremely subtle, like the time when a group of Communist officials walked into a Sunday school in the capital of Addis Ababa. They didn't disturb the meeting, but patiently waited until it was finished. Then one of them rose to speak.

"Children," the man said in a soft voice, "we want you all to take part in a nice demonstration in the square. Each one of you will get the gift of a toy gun. All we want you to do in return is to march like soldiers and learn a few slogans."

Naturally, a buzz of excitement swept through the room.

"Hands up all of you who'd like to come." Every hand shot up.

The believer who told me about this said that the Sunday school leaders were helpless and shed tears later that day as they saw their charges proudly marching along with thousands of other children, shouting parrot-fashion Communist slogans that they didn't understand.

The harsh truth is that the Christian teachers could not match the excitement that the Communists had offered their children. The comparison between the deadly dull Sunday school and the exhilarating occasion in the square caused many of the youngsters to leave for good and join an all-action Communist youth group.

All over Africa there is a need for a children's Bible to be produced in native language. It should have a selection of the major stories of the Bible, with lots of illustrations.

I remember the thrill I experienced when I was able to lead a group of four "smugglers" into one Marxist country with 300 copies of a children's Bible in a local African language.

Each of us carried boxes filled with Bibles from our car parked just short of the border. We proceeded along a winding bush trail to the stream which marked the border. We waded through the water and continued on towards a village we could see in the distance.

Suddenly we came face to face with a man who looked at us in great surprise.

"What do you have there?" he enquired.

"Children's Bibles," I replied.

"Can I have one?" he politely requested.

I prized open my box and handed him one. His eyes shone brightly as he scanned through it. "Wow. Wow." That's all he could say.

Suddenly children began to appear from everywhere and there at the side of the road we held an impromptu meeting. It wasn't long before all our precious cargo had been given away to those hungry people in that African village. God's Word was able to reach into their hearts. It was the first time most of them had ever seen a Bible.

### Practical Hints

1. For Parents:
   a. Give time and attention to your child. Don't let work and money dominate you. Your family is your greatest asset.
   b. Read the Bible (preferably a children's Bible) to your children and pray with them.
   c. Let them participate in activities such as Sunday school, youth meetings, etc.

    d. Talk to your minister and/or Sunday school leaders about the contents of the services.

    e. Become personally involved. There is a tremendous shortage of good and faithful workers.

2. For teachers:

    a. You have the children for the better part of the day. Accept your work as a calling from God.

    b. You are molding your children for an assignment in some office or company; also mold them spiritually.

    c. You give much time and attention to the child. Give time to God too — for personal Bible study and prayer. You cannot teach or guide the child beyond your own spiritual level.

It is important for parents, teachers and ministers to know what communism has to say about the education of the child: "It is important that each pupil, after he has completed his schooling, should become involved in the fight for a new world, the Communist world." Our children must indeed become involved, not with communism or capitalism but with the Kingdom of God. Parents, youth workers and the school play a most important role.

## Chapter 5

## POINTS FOR PERSONAL REFLECTION

1. Is our concern for the welfare of children like that shown by Jesus in Matthew 18:1-6,10-14?

2. Read Psalm 78:1-8. It expresses a divine principle, based on the command in Deuteronomy 6:6,7, that each generation has the obligation to teach its children the way of the Lord. How can we apply this in our family life?

3. An early training in godly principles is a basic foundation for maturity and growth. Note how Paul links that early training to the mature understanding of Timothy, as he describes the role of the Word of God in his life (2 Timothy 3:14-17).

## Chapter 6

# THE CHURCH OF THE FUTURE

What will the Church of the future be like? That is a very interesting question to which many answers have already been given. There will be revival and unity among the children of God, says one. There will be persecution, says another.

To define our subject we must differentiate between "the Church of the future" and "the future of the Church." We can argue over the Church of the future but not over the future of the Church. That future has been fixed. When Christ comes again, the whole church will undertake a space trip and meet her Lord in the air.

But what will the local churches look like before the Second Coming? Let me present a few thoughts:

1. I do not believe that the true church of Jesus Christ will ever become visibly one. Although Revelation speaks about an all-embracing world religion, there is no mention about a visible unity of born-again believers. The world religion will be a false one, and the true Church of Jesus Christ will be no part of it.

2. The church of the future will be less of an institutional church than it is today. Christians in communist countries gather in small groups. House churches have been formed, and the office of the believer has replaced the office of the minister to a great extent.

3. Countries which have been sending out missionaries will become mission fields themselves.

4. Missionary work will not be done by professional missionaries, but by laymen who will preach the gospel. If countries close their doors to mission work, then doctors, nurses, teachers and technicians will have to do the work of missionaries.

The above is speculative and therefore relative. The

Holy Spirit blows where He wills. He can change the situation in a moment. But the following is known to us from God's Word:

1. The gospel will be proclaimed to all nations before Christ's Second Coming. This does not mean all will be converted but that all nations will hear the gospel (Mark 13:10).

2. Many Christians will backslide. "And then many will fall away, and betray one another, and hate one another" (Matthew 24:10). They are not prepared to be persecuted or hated for the name of Jesus. The price of discipleship is too high. It is a sad thought that nominal Christians will hate and deliver one another up, hoping that in doing so they will escape persecution and death.

3. Because wickedness will increase, the love of many will grow cold. Love of God will be replaced by love of the world. It won't happen to a few Christians only, but to the majority. In the end times only a minority will remain faithful to the Lord (Matthew 24:12).

4. Christian persecution will increase worldwide (2 Timothy 3:12). That is why we must prepare. Only Christians who draw their strength from the Holy Spirit will be prepared to live and suffer for God and will remain steadfast. They will refuse to serve the world government and world religion, even though they know that their obedience to God will mean persecution, suffering and perhaps even death.

The Church of Christ will be a minority, but a conquering, overcoming minority. It might look as if we are losing the battle, but in fact we will be gaining the victory! Christians can therefore face the future fearlessly.

The above statements are not imaginative fiction but scriptural accounts of what will happen. There is hope for the future in spite of persecution. The Church of Christ is in fact the only group in the world which has a future. She never loses her members. "He who believes in me, though he die, yet shall he live" (John 11:25). We must think realistically — or, rather, biblically.

## House Churches

In countries where atheistic governments are in power and Christians are persecuted, many church buildings have been confiscated and nationalized. When the "Cultural Revolution" broke out in China in 1966, all churches and Christian schools were closed. But that did not mean the people of God were unable to meet. They met secretly in homes, and they still do. The size of these groups varies from place to place; sometimes only five to ten people gather, although sometimes there are many more. (In 1972, a Protestant church was opened in Peking, but only to serve the diplomatic community. Recently some registered churches have been opened in a number of major cities, but millions of Christians continue to meet in secret.)

In the province of Fukien hundreds of thousands of believers meet in more than 300 "house" groups. Their obedience to Christ is greater than their fear of the authorities. The forced existence of house churches has created a deep bond among Christians. The fellowship of the saints is thus experienced more intensely. Very little organization is needed. Believers of different denominations find their unity in Christ. There are no longer committee meetings, interdenominational differences or power politics. People no longer ask one another which church they belong to. The question is, "Do you belong to Jesus?" Traditional forms of service in these secret meetings have disappeared. Each Christian attends the service to serve and to share. "Church leadership" has purposely not been formalized because, in the event of police raids, the church leaders would be the first to be arrested.

Although witnessing or evangelizing in public is forbidden, Chinese Christians find ample opportunity to do so — even in a funeral service. A Chinese heathen custom calls for the beating of drums to ward off evil spirits of the dead. But a Christian funeral is different. Victory reigns, despite grief. While the funeral procession follows the hearse, the Christians sing hymns and songs of victory and faith.

If we want to prepare congregations for the future, we can learn from believers who have already lost their religious freedom, especially with regard to forming so-called "house churches." We need to analyze the pros and cons of these churches.

Before I do this, however, I would like to explain that the term "house church" is actually used within China. This term might not be acceptable in some countries; perhaps "house fellowship" would be more appropriate. Local churches need not fear that these fellowships will in any way rival the local congregation; instead they can be part of it. It is for this reason that we have to differentiate between house churches in Communist countries and house fellowships in free countries. We will discuss this later.

Let me analyze some advantages and disadvantages of "house churches" as compared to organized churches in Communist countries:

## Advantages of the House Church

| Churches | House Churches |
|---|---|
| 1. Only a few can take up the office of "minister" or "pastor." | 1. There is the "office of the believer." |
| 2. Large numbers allow little contact with one another. | 2. Close fellowship is experienced. |
| 3. Money is needed for salaries, church buildings and upkeep. | 3. No money is needed; no one receives a salary and there are no church buildings. |
| 4. Nominal Christians are not easily noticeable among the numbers. | 4. There are no nominal Christians. |
| 5. It is difficult for the gifts of the Spirit to function. | 5. The functioning of the gifts plays an essential part. |

| | |
|---|---|
| 7. The church needs much organization. | 7. There is little organization, more organism. |
| 8. Services are highly structured, with little variety. | 8. Variety occurs as all members take part in the service. |

## Disadvantages of the House Church

| **Churches** | **House Churches** |
|---|---|
| 1. Sacraments are maintained. | 1. Several of the sacraments disappear owing to the lack of leadership. |
| 2. No cliques are formed. | 2. The formation of cliques is an ever-present danger. |
| 3. Exposition of Scripture tends to be thorough. | 3. There is the danger of proclaiming personal opinions or false doctrine. |
| 4. Preaching tends to be more systematic; | 4. "Hobby" preaching (preaching about favorite topics) is a danger. |

It is obvious that a balance must be found. I do not want to pronounce any judgment, however; the advantages listed above speak for themselves. They are predominantly practical.

As far as the disadvantages are concerned, the position is slightly different. Here it concerns fundamental truths such as sacraments and exposition of Scripture. "House churches" do not give enough attention to these truths. Before we condemn the existence of these churches in Communist countries, however, it is interesting and important to investigate *why* these disadvantages are present.

Take, for example, the sacraments. A well-known Christian "China watcher" spoke about the situation of the churches in the People's Republic. When he mentioned the "house churches" he said that Communion was not observed because there were no ordained ministers to perform this duty. The most obvious conclusion would be, "You see, they don't even commemorate the Lord's Supper."

This problem is intensified among Catholics whose theological position is even more rigid on this point. Yet in the Ukraine, some four million believers have functioned as an underground community practicing the Catholic rites of priesthood, communion, baptism, etc. But all would agree that they had not been prepared for this possibility.

The question thus is: *Why* is Communion (and other sacraments) not observed? The answer is clear. Before the 1949 Red Revolution, the church in China followed the West's pattern. In the local church the minister kept a tight rein. He was the central figure; he alone served the sacraments. When the ministers were arrested, the Christians believed that no one was left to administer Communion.

Although Communion is usually served by a minister, must this be an exclusive service that can be performed only by him? Christ's instruction to remember His death would then depend on the presence of a minister. If the church in China had been prepared for their present situation, then the leader would have taught the congregation to observe the Lord's Supper without him.

China's situation is not unique. In many countries where atheist governments are in power, the same thing has happened. Everything revolved around the minister or the missionary. He preached, baptized and served Communion, and the congregation looked on. Then came the revolution. The missionaries fled the country, the local pastors were arrested and the congregation was unprepared.

## Courses for Spiritual Leadership

How can we prepare our churches in a practical way while there is religious freedom? How can the dangers introduced by "house churches" be transformed into advantages? What is there to learn from the advantages of the house churches in China? And how can we avoid small congregations springing up out of (and in conflict with) the local congregation? Let us put these matters in their proper order:

1. The church of the future will be confronted with persecution, apostasy, a world religion and a world government.

2. The church has to prepare for the difficult times lying ahead. It does not mean simply survival, however. We have to prepare churches not just to survive but to stand and to overcome despite circumstances.

3. Church members must become involved. The office of the believer in each church must be fully realized. "When you come together, each one has a hymn, a lesson a revelation ..." (1 Corinthians 14:26). Thus there is no "one-man show," as is sometimes the case now.

4. Although the sacraments should normally be served by those ordained in office, circumstances can necessitate an exception to the rule. Philip (a deacon) baptized the Ethiopian eunuch (Acts 8:38), and the above-mentioned examples taken from China speak for themselves.

Courses in spiritual leadership are necessary to prepare the church to function effectively in the future. Unlike individual "house churches," house fellowships can become an essential part of the local congregation. Elders should be trained by the local minister or pastor of the church to lead these fellowships. Alas, church committee meetings, which take up so much of a minister's time, are used mainly to discuss business and organizational problems. The minister's duties should not include only Sunday preaching and visitation, which leave little time for his church council which he needs to train spiritually. If he had more time, his deacons and elders could be instructed to teach the house fellowships.

If congregations were divided into districts, the elder overseeing each district could lead his own fellowship group. He knows the people in his area, their problems and their potential. The house fellowships can also, apart from Bible study, give time to intercessory prayer and testimonies. In this way all the members have an opportunity to contribute positively, "joined and knit together by every joint with which it is supplied, when each part is working properly . . ." (Ephesians 4:16). Under the leadership of a spiritual elder and the Holy Spirit, such a house fellowship will provide a positive contribution and blessing to the welfare of the whole local church during times of prosperity and freedom. And, should persecution come, they can continue to function, since they are not dependent on leaders or a minister.

House fellowships are flexible. In Eastern Europe, a majority of the believers attend regular worship services, but also participate in house meetings to supplement their spiritual diet. Natural celebrations of birthdays, namedays, weddings and funerals are all occasions for fellowship — often with hundreds present. This is a pattern which can be applied for all churches in the Western world. Make each visit to a believer's home a moment for worship, sharing of Scripture and prayer. As one Orthodox believer said of the Protestants in his country, "They always have to hold *meetings*!" We should follow suit! The Christian life is personal, not functional. It is for 24 hours a day. Too often we confine it to "meetings." Persecution will demand greater consistency in our use of time and greater flexibility in our concept of fellowship.

## Proof in the Eating

Sunday evening church meetings are often attended by only a few people. House fellowships could replace the evening service. It might sound revolutionary, but we must bear in mind that house fellowships are the only form of church structure that can survive a revolution.

There is a great need for personal contact among Christians. The house fellowship is an ideal solution, and the idea will work if we have enough vision for it. The effort required of the church council to organize a system of house fellowships will be a great blessing now and in the future.

The church of the future will then remain a strong living congregation which, because each member is involved, "... makes bodily growth and upbuilds itself in love" (Ephesians 4:16).

In September 1977 Idi Amin banned 27 Christian sects and denominations, permitting only Islam, Roman Catholicism, the Ugandan (Greek) Orthodox Church and the Church of Uganda (Anglican) to remain.

So the believers from the banned groups had a big decision to make. Should they join with the official churches, or should they form house fellowships? Within days of the ban, thousands of secret house fellowships had sprung up across the land. Baptists, Pentecostals and other denominations organized themselves so they could meet secretly in homes or in the forests.

One of the most amazing organizers of the Secret Church in Uganda was Ben Oluka, who became "God's double agent" in the President's office. He often used his access to secret documents to tip off believers who were about to be arrested. Even more dangerous, Oluka actually pastored a house fellowship in his own home. It was a small group from the Deliverance Church, an indigenous Ugandan evangelical fellowship.

Oluka says, "At the time, I was working in the office that had to enforce the president's ban, and secretly I was running a secret church myself.

"When the ban was announced, house meetings sprang up throughout the country. There is a higher power, and when government restricts the freedom of worship, God's supremacy has to take over.

"The free churches decided to follow the example of Acts 20:20, where the believers went from house to house breaking bread and worshipping God.

"This was a very trying time because anyone caught in one of these gatherings could easily be taken to the State Research Bureau.

"Many of the house fellowships were given names. Ours was called 'The Hill,' because that's where my home was — on top of the hill."

As well as the house meetings, the believers of Uganda had other ingenious ways of meeting for worship. Pastor Nicholas Wafula, the overseer of the banned Deliverance Church, explained: "When there was a wedding of one of our number, we would hold it in a Church of Uganda. We would all come together for the service and then the reception, which would be used as a time for worship and ministry. People would give testimonies, and the choir would sing. We also used birthday parties for the same purpose."

Probably the most unusual ruse the believers used was a furniture factory "church" in the Mengo district of Kampala. "The factory belongs to some of the brethren and they felt it was a perfect cover for them. At first the worshippers went through the factory as if to look at the furniture, through the banana grove, and into a nearby house. Finally the church became so large they also held meetings in the factory itself."

Since Amin's fall, church leaders from Ethiopia have been to Uganda to learn from their example. Now similar fellowships are springing up in Ethiopia.

Thousands of miles away, in the People's Republic of China, countless house churches had also sprung up after the terrible persecution by the Red Guards during the Cultural Revolution, when literally millions of Bibles were burnt in public and believers arrested and tortured.

Leader of one of the largest groups in China was "Mama" Kwang, an incredible woman of faith who was imprisoned three times for her activities, while her husband was also incarcerated in a labor camp. Her devoted ministry saw 300 house fellowships spring up.

Meetings were usually held every night, sometimes at 2 or 3 a.m.

Often their meetings happened without prior notice, frequently being called when Mrs. Kwang or one of her co-workers was led during prayer to hold one. On arrival at the destination she or the other preachers would be met by a crowd of believers waiting expectantly for their time of worship.

Whenever the preacher would ask how the group had been gathered, their reply was always the same: "The Lord Himself told us to come here for fellowship." No human method of communication had been used to gather them.

Often at these meetings, signs and miracles accompanied the preaching and worship. The dumb would be brought, and leave the place speaking. Blind people would leave seeing and the lame walking. All the time, the number of believers continued to grow.

Mrs. Kwang's son Daniel explained that the small fellowships would have just a few hundred members, while the big ones had thousands. They would often meet in large houses once owned by rich traders. The fellowship would split up into smaller groups and pack all the rooms of the mansion.

"It's the Lord's doing. He is very wonderful to us," said Daniel, a huge grin on his face.

So what is the secret of the faith of these Chinese believers, living as they do in such a hostile environment? Does their example mean that one has to be persecuted before having this kind of faith?

"No," Daniel said, "that is not the sacrifice. The sacrifice is *prayer*." For this reason, "house fellowships" are often called "prayer cells."

Chapter 6

## POINTS FOR PERSONAL REFLECTION

1. The Bible gives a number of illustrations of how believers should function together. Each of these pictures of the church has some added instruction for us. What can we learn from 1 Corinthians 12:27; Eph. 1:23, 4:16; and 1 Peter 2:5,9-10?

2. Our purpose in meeting together is to worship God, to celebrate the new and living relationship we have

through Jesus Christ, and also to interact with fellow
Christians. How are all of these brought together in
Hebrews 10:19-25?

3. The Apostle Paul found many places to preach and
teach. Note the variety in Acts 16:24,25; 16:40; 17:1,2;
17:17; 17:22; 18:7; 19:9; 20:7,8; 21:5,6. What are the advantages and disadvantages of each of these situa-
tions?

4. How would your church prepare if you knew persecution were coming to your country soon?

**Chapter 7**

# SPIRITUAL OR CAPABLE LEADERS?

"So I took the heads of your tribes, wise and experienced men, and set them as heads over you ..." (Deuteronomy 1:15).

"Pick out from among you seven men of good repute, full of the Spirit and of wisdom, whom we may appoint to this duty" (Acts 6:3).

There is an important difference between the two verses quoted above. A nation should have wise and experienced men, who are capable to rule, to be appointed over them. God's people, the Church, however, should have people who are not only capable and wise but also especially filled with the Holy Spirit. They must be *spiritually* capable. In the appointing of elders and deacons this should be the first requirement.

When God calls men to an office in the Church, He does not look at the position they hold in society. Neither does He care that they have a university degree. The Lord seeks men filled with the Holy Spirit. He looks for *spiritual* leaders.

The danger exists in our churches today that not enough attention is given to this requirement. Consequently we look for the more academically capable men instead of spiritual men. The requirements laid down by Moses were related to a task which was to lead a nation. Other standards are required to fill an office in the Church of Christ. No purely natural leaders are needed here, but spiritual men of God.

## A Drunk Elder

The church was full. The internationally-known evangelist remained in the vestry together with an almost complete church council. Everyone was agitated. The

head elder had not turned up. The reason for his absence
was that he had attended a wedding reception the previous night and had drunk too much. He had stayed in bed
with a hangover. It caused much consternation. How
could this possibly happen, especially since there was a
guest speaker from abroad?

Suddenly the visiting preacher asked if he might say
something. His words filled the whole church council with
surprise. He asked if such an occurrence, in which an
elder neglected his duty for the same reason, had taken
place before. They all shook their heads. They even pro-
posed that the elder should be discharged from his office.
The evangelist nodded in agreement.

"You are right," he said. "Anyone who is a drunkard
cannot be an elder. Ephesians 5:18 makes this clear."

The elders and deacons nodded in assent.

"It is an order from the Lord that we may not be drunk
with wine," he added. "But it is also an order that we
should be filled with the Holy Spirit. Those who have not
fulfilled this condition can be neither elders nor deacons."

An embarrassed silence followed.

"May I ask who of you are filled with the Holy Spirit?"
asked the evangelist.

No one answered. Shamefully they hung their heads.

"This means that not one of you can fill the position of
elder or deacon this morning," the evangelist concluded.

It was obvious. The requirement God demands for the
office of an elder in the church may never be taken too
lightly. God wants men with a good testimony, full of wisdom and the Holy Spirit, to be appointed. Only they will
be able to lead the Church of God. The same principle
applies to the minister or pastor. If a vacancy exists in a
church, it is the duty of the Church Council to appoint a
minister who is filled with the Holy Spirit.

I doubt if many churches would have considered Paul
for the office of minister based on his own personal testimony: "When I came to you, brethren, I did not come proclaiming to you the testimony of God in lofty words or
wisdom" (1 Corinthians 2:1). We skate on thin ice when
lofty words and wisdom are considered to be the only
qualifications to fill the positions of office bearers in a

church. Paul's qualification lay in his weakness: "And I was with you in weakness and in much fear and trembling; and my speech and my message were not in plausible words of wisdom ..." (1 Corinthians 2:3,4). When Paul spoke, there was no reaction of, "What a good speaker," or "He captivates the audience when he speaks."

The things we consider to be a recommendation, Paul rejected. He came in weakness, fear and trembling. He admitted that his own preaching did not contain plausible words of wisdom. "But," he added, "in demonstration of the Spirit and of power, that your faith might not rest in the wisdom of men but in the power of God" (1 Corinthians 2:4-5).

## Weak People — Powerful Leaders

There is a great need for spiritual leaders. In Laos we made the mistake which is so often made: we appointed capable leaders as elders instead of spiritual people. We accepted people who could read and write. (In Laos eighty percent of the nation is illiterate.) When the Communists took over Laos, many "capable" leaders denied the Lord. The spiritual people were the ones who remained faithful.

A spiritual leader is a person whose power is acknowledged in heaven, on earth and in hell. These leaders are sought after by God today.

Jesus chose simple fishermen, not those from the Sanhedrin, to represent His Kingdom. "When they saw the boldness of Peter and John, and perceived that they were uneducated, common men, they wondered; and they recognized that they had been with Jesus. But seeing the man that had been healed standing beside them, they had nothing to say in opposition" (Acts 4:13-14).

Peter and John did not belong to the Sanhedrin, but they had qualifications which the Pharisees (the "qualified" leaders) did not have. They had been with Jesus and were filled with the Holy Spirit. That was the qualification. The proof was the man who had been healed. They could not have anything against this. When the excited crowd gathered around them, Peter did not claim honor for himself but asked them, "Why do you stare at us, as though by our own power or piety we had made him walk?" (Acts 3:12).

"For consider your call, brethren; not many of you were wise according to worldly standards, not many were powerful, not many were of noble birth; but God chose what is foolish in the world to shame the wise, God chose what is weak in the world to shame the strong, God chose what is low and despised in the world, even things that are not, to bring to nothing things that are, so that no human being might boast in the presence of God" (1 Corinthians 1:26-29).

God chooses His ambassadors from this group. Through being filled with the Holy Spirit, people who know they are weak in themselves are made powerful men of God. They do not touch their honor and glory, but give it to Him who reveals His strength in the weak. "When I am weak, then I am strong" (2 Corinthians 12:10). "I will all the more gladly boast of my weaknesses, that the power of Christ may rest upon me. For the sake of Christ, then, I am content with weaknesses . . ." (2 Corinthians 12:9-10).

Brother Andrew recently applied to join the "Not Terribly Good Club" of Great Britain. He wanted public recognition that he was a failure. The club had been set up by British eccentric Stephen Pile, for people who had dismally failed in many different ways.

In his letter of application to Pile, Andrew explained that, when he first came to Britain in 1954 for his missionary training, he stayed with William Hopkins, whom he eventually came to affectionately know as Uncle Hoppy.

"Uncle Hoppy had a storefront mission hall in Gravesend, Kent, and would insist that I preach even though he was the only other person there," laughed "God's Smuggler."

"I was a complete failure because no one came to hear me preach. We would take up the offering, have the reading, and give the announcements, and still the place would be empty."

Brother Andrew also confessed to the times when he had been a failure in smuggling Bibles through the Iron Curtain. He told of the occasion when he was caught at

the border with his cargo of Scriptures and interrogated.
"This is more proof of my failure," he wrote.

Brother Andrew confessed that he really wanted to
join the club mainly so that he could become its chaplain
and preach about Jesus, who "to many was the biggest
failure in history." Andrew added, "He died a criminal's
death — and so it seemed his life was a complete failure."

"But was it really?" he asks. "By His resurrection, He
turned apparent failure into success. That is what I
wanted to show to those who think they are failures."

"God uses the weak things of this world to confound
the wise."

Sadly, Brother Andrew was not able to join the club.
The founder, Stephen Pile, has had to disband it because
of the success of his book, *The Book of Heroic Failures*,
which is now a *bestseller*!

A spiritual leader is someone who sees further than his
own organization or church. He is concerned about the
whole Kingdom of God and not just his own little kingdom. He isn't trying to build his own organization and
name, but God's. I see that quality very much in Brother
Andrew.

Another man who had a similar character was Lung
Singh, a former opium addict from Laos who came to
know Christ as his Savior after being addicted for 45
years. This man was completely sold out to the Lord. He
grew so quickly that believers often sought his counsel on
spiritual matters rather than going to more "capable"
and better educated leaders. For the people saw Christ in
him.

I baptized Lung Singh in the Mekong River in Laos and
I'll never forget how, after coming up out of the waters,
he began singing, "I have decided to follow Jesus." Then
he pointed to the ripples spreading out in the water and
said, "Brother Jan, there goes my old life. All the old
things have passed away. It's gone. Everything now is
new."

Still soaking wet, he clambered onto the bank on the
side of the famous river and knelt down. "Devil," he
shouted, "I've been your servant for 45 years. Now I belong to Christ. Now I serve only him."

I've never met a man so on fire for the Lord. After I left the country in 1973, Lung Singh continued his courageous ministry. He was constantly warned by the Pathet Lao to stop his preaching, but he refused.

"I cannot do that. Jesus saved me. He did everything for me. I can't be quiet," he said.

Three years after I left the country, he was arrested and taken out into a forest, where he was executed.

Lung Singh was not, in the eyes of men, a great administrator; but he was a spiritual leader qualified by God Himself. He was faithful unto death because he listened to the voice of the Holy Spirit and was a man of the Book. He was a man big in the eyes of God.

## Francis of Assisi

Francis of Assisi, the Italian friar who in 1209 founded a religious order, discovered the secret of success. On a certain day some men approached him and asked how he managed to do such a great work for God. Francis, who had laid down rules which required chastity, poverty, and obedience, and laid special stress on preaching and ministration to the sick, smiled and said:

"It is very simple. One day God told His angels to go to earth and look for a man who would be able to do a great work for Him. The angels carried out the instructions and returned a little while later to God. They had found the man with all the necessary qualifications. He was a very experienced and learned man. God rejected their choice. He found the man too capable. 'He will claim all the honor for himself,' God told the angels, 'and the people will think he was able to do the work because he was so capable.' "

Francis went on to say, "Then God sent the angels out with the order to look for an insignificant man. They searched and searched, but always returned with the wrong man. Finally the Lord told them to look for a man who was despised and a fool in the eyes of the world.

"Eventually the angels found a man who was nothing in the eyes of the people. 'This is my man,' said the Lord God. 'He is so weak and insignificant that the people will know immediately that he could never do the work in his own power. They will give me all the honor.' "

Francis looked earnestly at the men and said, "I was that man." God does not want to share His honor (Isaiah 42:8). He looks for people who are nothing in themselves, so that His power can be fully revealed. They will be the spiritual leaders, because they know their capability is in Christ Jesus.

If we want to prepare our churches for times of persecution, we will have to follow these biblical principles. We need spiritual people to do spiritual work. The capable people can handle the business side of the work, such as administration, organization and finances. That is not an inferior service; good organization in a church is necessary. It is part of the whole and promotes growth. Problems exist, however, when more attention is given to organization than to the spiritual growth of the church.

## Sardis and Laodicea

The churches of Sardis and Laodicea were well-organized. Services were well-attended, the collections fantastic and everyone in the vicinity spoke highly of these good churches. "Ours is a lively church," said the people of Sardis. And those of Laodicea added, "Ours is a rich church, one that fulfills its obligations." Apparently these were two model churches, an example to the whole area. The financial committees would return from the synod with compliments. "In comparison to Smyrna and Philadelphia, our financial position is good," the committees would report back.

In God's eyes this was not considered a sign of life. "I know your works; you have the name of being alive, and you are dead" (Revelation 3:1). That was God's opinion of the church of Sardis.

The church at Laodicea didn't fare too well either. "For you say, I am rich, I have prospered, and I need nothing; not knowing that you are wretched, pitiable, poor, blind, and naked" (Revelation 3:17). The rich, successful church of Laodicea did not even have a place for the Lord, although they preached about Him. The Lord stood on the outside of His own church: "Behold, I stand at the door and knock . . ." (Revelation 3:20).

The Lord advised the Laodicean church to buy salve for their eyes, that they may see their need (Revelation 3:18). We need this salve today. We deceive ourselves and our churches by becoming so organized that we consider ourselves alive. During times of need and persecution, the organizational side will fall away. The examples given of the church in China make this clear. The spiritual power can remain, because it does not depend on committees, buildings, collections or even office bearers. It is the power of the Holy Spirit in the believer's heart which is the decisive factor.

The church of Sardis was believed to be alive but the fact is that it was spiritually dead. The church of Philadelphia appeared weak and poor, but the Lord's opinion was, "You have but little power, and yet you have kept my word and have not denied my name" (Revelation 3:8). The church at Smyrna received the same compliment: "I know your tribulation and your poverty (but you are rich) . . ." (Revelation 2:9). The meaning is clear: The church was rich in its faith in God. That is why the Lord tells the church of Smyrna, "Do not fear what you are about to suffer" (Revelation 2:10). And to the faithful church at Philadelphia he says, "Because you have kept my word of patient endurance, I will keep you from the hour of trial which is coming on the whole world . . ." (Revelation 3:10).

The Lord does not promise a future without persecution, but He promises victory in the hour of persecution and suffering. Those who wait expectantly on the Lord will be kept in the hour of temptation.

## Natural and Spiritual Leadership

The late U.S. President, Harry S Truman, described a natural leader as "a person who possesses the ability to make others do something they themselves would not like to do, and actually enjoy doing it."

Li Hung Chang, an old Chinese leader, phrased it this way: "There are three types of people: those who are movable, those who are immovable, and those who are able to move others. The latter are the leaders."

Oswald Sanders, former General Director of the Overseas Missionary Fellowship, said that spiritual leadership derived from a combination of natural and spiritual qualifications. Natural ability is also a gift from God. It is not through his own natural capabilities that a spiritual leader exercises his influence on his surroundings, but through the power of the Holy Spirit. A self-made spiritual leader does not exist. It is through the working of the Holy Spirit giving His gifts to weak men, so that they can become powerful leaders in the household of God. It is not the crown but the cross which is relevant to spiritual leaders. They have learned to reiterate John the Baptist's words: "He must increase, but I must decrease" (John 3:30).

Natural and spiritual leadership corresponds, but there is a difference. It is clearly set out hereunder:

| Natural leaders | Spiritual leaders |
| --- | --- |
| Self-confidence | Confidence in God |
| Makes his own decisions | Seeks the leading of the Holy Spirit |
| Knows his people | Knows his God |
| Always thinking out new plans | Only wants to know the plan of God |
| Keen to give orders | Carries out God's orders with joy |
| Has many subordinates | Is everyone's servant |
| Independent | Dependent on God |
| Demands that others listen to him | Listens to God and obeys Him |
| Reaches toward greater achievements | Always seeks to decrease |
| Ponders much | Prays much |

The words disciple and discipline stem from the same word. Only a spiritual leader will have followers as he submits himself to the discipline of the mighty hand of God.

Problems are created when people only want to be leaders and not followers. It reminds me of the little boys who were playing war on a street. A passer-by asked them why they were doing nothing and why it was so quiet. One little boy answered, "We were all generals. No one wants to be a soldier and fight."

## People With Vision

Spiritual leaders are people with vision — a vision of God and a vision of the world. Because of God's victory they can venture ahead. They are optimistic instead of pessimistic.

A pessimist will never be able to be a spiritual leader, because pessimism is unbelief. The pessimist sees a problem in each opportunity.

The optimist sees an opportunity in each problem. He knows that our problems are God's plans. Because he has a vision, he makes himself available to carry out the vision. He does not wait for help so that someone else can do the work for him, but does it himself.

Studying church or mission history, one cannot help but be impressed with the vision the spiritual leaders had. They received their orders and immediately started to work on them, whether they had helpers or not. It is for this reason that they often stood alone and were lonely people. They were not always understood, but they carried on, despite the consequences.

The person with a vision must put it into practice, or else he remains but a dreamer instead of a leader. When a spiritual leader receives insight into God's will, then he must get into motion, whatever the results may be. To achieve his aim he must be willing to burn his boats behind him. When the Romans set foot on English soil, their first order was to burn all the boats in which they had sailed. Their vision was: Forward! The road back was made impossible.

A certain young man who had joined the Coast Guard was put to the test when a violent storm sprang up. A ship had sent out distress signals. On entering the lifeboat the young man was frightened by the gigantic waves and in his anxiety shouted to the captain. "We will never be able to return, Captain!" Back over the waves came the captain's reply: "We need never come back. We must sail out!"

That was Martin Luther's approach, too. The German Protestant reformer feared neither man nor Pope. He wanted to obey only God and His Word. When Luther received word that he was to defend himself at the Diet of Worms, his friends advised him not to go. "Not go?" Luther exclaimed indignantly. "Of course I am going to Worms, even if I have to meet as many devils as there are tiles on the roofs."

## Vision or Visa

In Open Doors our aim is to aid the Suffering Church. Some years ago now, a young man from Holland, Brother Andrew, received his vision. When Andrew was twenty-five, God called him to help the Suffering Church in Communist countries. Youthful though he was, he already displayed the qualities of a spiritual leader. He had no money, but he had faith in God.

Instead of waiting for necessary funds and helpers, he traveled alone to Eastern Europe in a little Volkswagen. The "capable leaders" all shook their heads. "You should be better organized and financed," they advised. But because he was obedient to God, Brother Andrew decided to go on his own.

"You will never return alive," some "wise men" admonished him.

"I don't have to," was Brother Andrew's reply. "The Lord never told me to come back. He just told me to *go*."

Andrew had another motto: "If you want to work *for* God, appoint a committee; but if you want to work *with* God, you only need a prayer group."

That is why he visited all his prayer partners and asked if they would pray for him. They did. They laid hands on him and sent him off. He departed for Eastern Europe, without money or financial guarantee, but with a mighty God.

Now twenty-five years later he is still working with God — not only now to Communist countries in Eastern Europe but to every area of the world where Christians suffer for their faith. "Our problem is that, too often, we want to carry out God's orders on condition that we will return safely from the dangerous areas," says Brother Andrew.

Yes, that is still our greatest problem. But obedience without willingness to make sacrifices is not obedience.

One of the offices of Open Doors is in Johannesburg, South Africa. The Suffering Church in Africa is aided and supplied with the Word of God from there. Nearly every week teams leave for Mozambique, Zimbabwe, Ethiopia and Angola. Because white South Africans cannot get visas for some of the above countries, Africans are used as couriers. They cross the borders unnoticed.

But a white South African employee of Open Doors tried to get a visa once. He received a telexed reply from the Frelimo government in Mozambique. The message was in Portuguese. He did not know the language and assumed the telex would suffice as a visa. I discussed his plan of travel with him before his departure. He had a particular mission to carry out in Mozambique, with a few specific instructions. He left Johannesburg by plane and on his arrival in Maputo presented the telex to the immigration officer.

The official looked at him inquiringly. "Where is your visa?"

"In your hand," the white South African answered and pointed to the telex.

"This is not a visa," the man replied. "It is a telex advising you that you cannot come now, but that you might be allowed to come later."

The result was that he had to return to Johannesburg, but there was no flight back until the next day. The Frelimo government representative did not want to create a bad impression, so he decided to take the South African to a hotel in Maputo, where he would stay for the next twenty-four hours. "The Frelimo government will pay all expenses," he was told.

Our courier was transported to Maputo and back in a police car — in other words, a day's sojourn in Maputo free. He was fortunate in that he was allowed to move about freely in the Mozambican capital during his twenty-four hours of "imprisonment." In this short time he was able to carry out all the orders which had been assigned to him. He returned a day later. On meeting him, I found him smiling broadly.

"Orders carried out," he said. "Everything went according to plan."

According to plan . . . When God gives orders, He opens doors — with or without a visa. The only condition? Be ready to go and perhaps never return.

Another Open Doors employee went to Mozambique with me a little while ago at the request of a group of Christians there. We went as far as the border by motor car, and from there the seventy-three-year-old co-worker and I crossed the Mozambican border on foot.

It was a dangerous venture for two whites — one a South African minister. The actual border crossing was a stream. There were no guard posts; at least none was seen. The journey was difficult; uphill, downhill, deeper into Mozambique. It was dangerous, the more so because a man had been murdered the previous day in that area. Frelimo soldiers were everywhere. Any shrub could have concealed one of them, but it never entered our minds. Our thoughts were with the Christians awaiting our arrival beyond the next hill.

Eventually we saw the village. The Christians were on the lookout for us. As soon as they spotted us they waved their hands, and we received a hearty welcome.

Suddenly another man walked toward us. "It is the Frelimo representative for our area," one of the Christians said. What was his intention? The Frelimo representative was so surprised that a white man had come walking over the hill. But he did not arrest us. Instead he gave the white South African minister a bunch of bananas! The Christians' faces beamed with joy and happiness. Even the Frelimo man stayed to attend the meeting.

Christians came from all directions to greet us. They slaughtered a goat for a feast in honor of their guests. It was a remarkable experience.

The meaning is clear. You don't necessarily need a visa. But you do need a vision and faith. And, of course, the willingness to be caught. "To wait for a visa takes too much time," the South African minister said. "My visa is in Matthew 28:19: '*Go* therefore!'" And he added with a little laugh, "That visa is two thousand years old, but is still valid today."

That is how a spiritual leader talks. He will remain steadfast in times of persecution because during the times of freedom he was prepared to suffer for the name of Jesus.

"But I do not account my life of any value nor as precious to myself, if only I may accomplish my course and the ministry which I received from the Lord Jesus, to testify to the gospel of the grace of God" (Acts 20:24).

Chapter 7

## POINTS FOR PERSONAL REFLECTION

1. Peter laid down an early test of leadership qualifications in Acts 6:3, when the church had to select the first set of deacons. How was this early, simple description expanded in 1 Timothy 3:8-13?

2. Paul possessed many natural abilities, but he understood their proper role in leading people to Christ. Apply his analysis, in 1 Corinthians 2:1-5, to your own life and witness.

3. The lettters to the churches recorded in Revelation 2 and 3 are addressed to the leaders of those churches. Examine these letters closely in order to see the quality of spiritual leadership, or lack of it, within these churches. Do these qualities and failures apply today?

# CHRISTIANS PERSECUTING CHRISTIANS

"I know that after my departure fierce wolves will come in among you, not sparing the flock; and from among your own selves will arise men speaking perverse things, to draw away the disciples after them" (Acts 20:29-30).

The worst kind of persecution is Christians who persecute Christians. It sounds dreadful, but it is true.

The Bible gives repeated warnings. They will "betray one another and hate one another" (Matthew 24:10). What a sad thought, and this will increase as the end times draw near. Many Christians, hoping to avoid persecution and save their own lives, will betray their fellow Christians. Not only does this apply to the end times, which we'll discuss in this chapter, but it is already happening.

Jesus Christ was not condemned by the Romans but the "pious" Jews, Pharisees, chief priests and scribes. They hated Him although He proclaimed the same God, the God of Abraham, Isaac and Jacob. The reason they hated Him was simple: their positions were threatened. The people followed Jesus instead of them. To prevent their self-established kingdom from falling, they decided to murder Jesus. Even Pilate realized that the chief priests delivered Jesus up because they were envious (Mark 15:10). Pilate, even though a heathen, wanted to protect Jesus from these "pious" Jews who demanded His death.

The apostles also experienced the same persecution. Although they were sent into a heathen world, they were persecuted by the religious Jews. They were thrown out of the temples and synagogues only to be later thrown into prisons.

The first martyr was a deacon, Stephen. Saul, the religious Jew, looked after the clothes of his fellow Jews so that they could move more freely while stoning Stephen. "And on that day a great persecution arose against the church in Jerusalem ... But Saul laid waste the church, and entering house after house, he dragged off men and women and committed them to prison" (Acts 8:1,3). The pious Saul had only one aim: to murder the Christians. "For you have heard ... how I persecuted the church of God violently and tried to destroy it" (Galatians 1:13).

## Arius and Athanasius

As if their very lives depended on it, Arius and Athanasius fought one another in the Fourth Century. Although we reject Arius' doctrine, it is sad that these two men could not come to some agreement between them. The world at that time was so shaken by this dispute between Bishop Arius and Deacon Athanasius that the emperor, Constantine, had to intervene between these two fighting men. In the year 325 he called a Council of Prelates together in Nicaea, in the northwestern part of Asia Minor. More than three hundred bishops attended.

It was an impressive meeting. Several bishops still bore the scars of torture received during former persecutions. Deacon Athanasius won the battle. As he was not yet a bishop, he was not allowed in the synod hall. What could he teach the wise men inside? They could do without him, they thought.

Fortunately, Athanasius had a few friends among the bishops. As soon as Arius had voiced his opinion that Jesus was not the same being as the Father but was the highest creation, a few of the bishops went to Athanasius to tell him of Arius' allegations. "What do we answer on your behalf?" they asked. Athanasius then gave his reply, and the bishops hurried back into the synod hall. A little while later they came to Athanasius with a few more questions. Athanasius gave his answers, and they quickly disappeared into the hall again.

In this manner Athanasius won the dispute. The church doctrine decreed that Jesus was "one in being" (in the Greek, *homo-ousios*) with the Father and not, as Arius maintained, "same in being" (in the Greek, *homoi-ousios*).

One letter made the difference. It was a very important difference too. Bishop Arius was expelled and Deacon Athanasius was made Bishop of Alexandria three years later, in 328.

Sixty years later, at the Council of Constantinople, Athanasius' view was approved, and the canonical doctrine of the Trinity established. Our well-known confession of faith, the Nicene Creed, descends from this Council at Nicaea. Although one is thankful that Athanasius won the dispute, it still remains regrettable that Christians can be so at variance with one another that an emperor has to intervene.

The battle between Christians was not over. They fought and persecuted one another again and again. It became so bad that, at one time, no mission work or evangelizing was done. Church leaders were too busy with domestic affairs. One council followed another. Each council appointed committees of inquiry. Church strife, disputes and hatred constituted the order of the day.

Mohammed was born during this time. He derided the Christians and reproached them because of their divisions. His motto, "Allah is God and Mohammed is his prophet," drew the masses. The Christianized countries of North Africa were tired of power politics and feuding within the church. Mohammed directed a tremendous mission offensive and a new religion took root in the hearts of millions: Islam. As a result of hatred among Christians, which caused persecution and suffering, a new religion was born.

Islam still displays that same tremendous mission drive today. While it gained ground then because of division among Christians, today it influences the world because of the power of the "oil god." The Western world will do anything for this "god"; it has resulted in some Protestant churches in Western Europe taking up collections for the building of mosques. The church which makes this compromise with Islam will also reap bitter fruit in the future.

Communist governments also have been adroit at exploiting divisions in the Church. One of the saddest disputes to take place in modern times is that between

China's official Protestant church, the Three-Self Movement, and Wang Ming-Dao, one of the country's most famous Christians.

Wang Ming-Dao is now an old man. Prior to the 1949 Communist Revolution he, along with Watchman Nee, had been a major leader of the Chinese Church. Even after Mao had seized power, Wang Ming-Dao continued preaching to large crowds, and his writings were widely circulated throughout China.

But it didn't last, and finally this courageous believer was arrested and has spent 23 years in prison for his faith.

Mr. Wang began preaching in 1921 and his church in Peking — the Christian Tabernacle — was regularly packed out. He also set up a Bible school in the capital.

But as far as the state-controlled Three-Self Movement was concerned, Wang Ming-Dao was a stubborn man. Not only was he uncompromising in regard to salvation itself, but also in relation to the life-style of the committed Christian; he affirmed it must reflect a purity straight from the heart of the Lord Himself.

When the Three-Self Movement was set up in the early fifties, it called for all Protestant churches to throw off the control of "Imperialist influences" from the West, and thus adhere to the "self-propagating" requirement of the official church.

Because Wang Ming-Dao had begun his own church himself, he could not see any reason to join with the movement — his group had been of Chinese origins all along.

But his attitude was not acceptable to the authorities. They wanted to have complete control of all religious life in China, despite claims of freedom, and would tolerate no exceptions.

A huge criticism meeting was called to force Wang Ming-Dao and his wife to change their minds. But to no avail. In 1955 both husband and wife were taken to prison and the unwavering voice of Peking's largest church was silenced.

In prison, Wang Ming-Dao was subjected to constant torture and brainwashing, until after 14 months, he finally signed a confession that his opposition to the Three-Self Movement had been "counter-revolutionary." After his release, he was deeply disturbed emotionally about his actions, and finally concluded that they had been brought about by the brainwashing itself.

He rejected his "confession," and was immediately returned to prison. This time he was to remain 21 years and 8 months. In January 1980, he was released again. In Shanghai, he was reunited with his wife, who had been freed two years earlier.

Open Doors leaders in Asia met him in China in 1980, shortly after his release. One of them recalls, "When I met with him, it would not have surrpised me to find a quiet, aging man, perhaps somewhat broken in body and with the same determination for his Lord that I had read about all these years.

"The signs of old age were naturally there, with his very limited vision and hearing — and yet for a man of 80 years who had undergone so much, he was in surprisingly strong health."

This godly brother was then asked if he had any message for the outside world. In reply, he talked about the verses which had sustained him in prison:

"I remember the words of Jesus to His Church in Revelation 2:10, 'Do not fear what you are about to suffer. Behold, the devil is about to throw some of you into prison, that you may be tested, and for ten days you will have tribulation. Be faithful unto death, and I will give you the crown of life.'

"So I have been through 23 years of refining and the Lord has not allowed me to suffer loss through it all, but rather to receive an even greater blessing."

The hearts of the Open Doors team went out to this great teacher who had endured so much, as he agonized over what he called his "fall."

"Twenty-five years ago, I felt that I was very stable, very strong. I had not fallen for 30 years. I'd preached the Gospel and not fallen. But I'd forgotten that Satan was waiting to use my weakest point to attack me.

"Satan took advantage of my timidity to attack me. 'Aren't you afraid?' he said. And he brought me face to

face with a terror that I had never even conceived of before. Never in my life had I confronted anything so fear-
some, and I, like Peter, was weak.

"My weakness and falling away was just like Peter's,
because he saw our Lord there suffering whipping and
mocking and was afraid that he would be in for the same
fate.

"Well, what happened in the end? After the Lord rose
from the dead, he appeared first of all to this fallen Peter.
Now my Lord has done the same with me. Not only has
He not remonstrated with me, but instead He has comforted me."

He added, "Now there is only one thing I fear. What is
that thing? I fear God. So long as I do not sin against God,
so long as I remain faithful to Him, then I fear nothing."

To Wang Ming-Dao, whose name means "Witness to
the Truth," it is critical that Christians understand his
need to hold fast to his Lord.

"There is an ancient Chinese saying, 'There are many
beginnings but few endings.' Everybody doing anything
makes a start, but those who carry through to the end
and complete it are very few."

He went on, "Ahead God is leading, and behind me God
is defending. I am in the middle. What have I to fear?"

One of those present commented, "I had been sitting in
an armchair beside Wang Ming-Dao throughout the afternoon, but to me it seemed I was sitting at his feet as he delivered his probing exhortation."

"Witness to the truth" he undoubtedly was. His fire for
the Lord had remained unchanged, and even 23 years of
persecution and suffering had been powerless to quench
it.

Wang Ming-Dao's problems stemmed directly from the
opposition of a hostile government. But opposition can
come from friendly quarters, too. In Laos, dear Brother
Soeban suffered bitter persecution at the hands of some
of the missionaries. I am sure his charismatic personality
was too much for some of them and they were constantly
sniping at him and his ministry with sarcastic remarks.

One day I asked this dear man, "Soeban, when will Laos
see revival?"

He looked at me with sadness in his eyes. "Brother Jan, it will only take place when the missionaries here get right with one another."

He was right.

## The Murder of the Huguenots

Protestantism took root in France amid bloody persecution. The Huguenots, as the Christians were called, accepted the Calvinistic confession of faith. The Roman Catholic church vehemently opposed this and plotted to murder the Huguenots.

Henry of Navarre was to marry Margaretha of Valois, King Charles X's sister. All the Huguenot leaders were invited to the wedding. King Charles had devised a plan to murder the Huguenots at the wedding. To protect himself, he appointed his mother, Catherine de Medici, to give the necessary murder signal.

The night of St. Bartholomeus on August 24, 1572, was a terrible night. Five thousand Huguenots were murdered at the "wedding feast," and that was only the beginning. Within the next five days, more than fifty thousand Christians were killed in cold blood in the whole of France.

The messenger who brought the news to the Pope was rewarded with a gift of one thousand crowns. The Pope shouted, "Good news, good news!" Guns were fired at the castle of St. Angelo and bonfires lit in the streets. To commemorate this event, the Pope had a medal made with the following words: "The massacre of the Huguenots." The Huguenots who managed to escape fled abroad.

King Charles of France experienced the truth of Proverbs 17:13, "If a man returns evil for good, evil will not depart from his house." In his last hours he suffered a dreadful death-struggle, dying at the age of twenty-four. "The wicked plots against the righteous, and gnashes his teeth at him; ... The wicked draw the sword ... to slay those who walk uprightly; ... their sword shall enter their own heart ..." (Psalm 37:12,14,15).

## Church Strife

We should search our own hearts before we point
fingers at the Roman Catholic church. We ignore those
who do not belong to "our church" or classify them as sec-
tarians. Every Sunday we very piously recite the creed,
"I believe in the fellowship of the saints," but add our own
interpretation: the fellowship of the saints in *our* church.
Those who do not belong to *our* church cannot have fellowship with us; the foundation of unity is not Jesus but
the church as an institution. That is a dangerous tendency
and is also unscriptural. We make the very big mistake
Paul warns us about: "One says, 'I belong to Paul,' and
another, 'I belong to Apollos'" (1 Corinthians 3:4). What
would Paul have to say about our division? The same as
he told the Corinthians: "You are still of the flesh"
(1 Corinthians 3:3).

Do I advocate one national church? Or should I rather
speak about unity in diversity? I would rather accept the
latter, but I am afraid it will remain just a slogan, that in
practice there will be more diversity than unity.

"We don't have to sacrifice our own identity," argued a
brother once. It depends on what you understand about
"our own identity." If you have died with Christ, if the old
has passed away, if you are a new creation (Galatians 2:20
and 2 Corinthians 5:17), then very little will be left of your
own identity. Then there remains only one form of true
unity: "We regard no one from a human point of view . . .
Therefore, if any one is in Christ, he is a new creation; the
old has passed away, behold, the new has come. All this is
from God, who through Christ reconciled us to Himself
. . ." (2 Corinthians 5:16-18). According to the Bible, the
fellowship of the saints does not come to a full stop at
your church; it starts there.

In facing difficult times ahead, we cannot take the
luxurious liberty of fighting against one another. We
need each other, especially in times of need. If the love of
Christ is poured out in our hearts, then we can look at our
brother in another church, offer him the hand of fellowship and experience that we belong to the *one* family of

God. Hence it is not necessary to become one great national church.

This requires a spiritual unity which must become visible in a practical way. "See how they love one another" should be the reaction of the world. This is more important than, "See how they congregate in one building." Unity was born in China through oppression and persecution. The buildings disappeared and unity was formed.

One of the lessons of the Suffering Church in Eastern Europe was to learn how to love even the fellow believers who became the unwitting tools of Communist oppression. For many years the Soviet Baptists have been split into registered and unregistered churches. The leaders of the two groups are mutually offended by one another, though there are men of God on both sides. Yet a wonderful thing is happening among the young people, many of whom find fellowship in both camps. Forgiveness and love will always root out the potential bitter division which Satan tries to sow among the believers.

## The Lesson From Uganda

Among the countries of Africa, Uganda is not only one of the most beautiful — Winston Churchill once described it as "the Pearl of Africa" — but also one of the most Christianized. Eighty percent of the population is Christian. During the years of spiritual revival, Christians would greet one another with the words, "Do you still walk in the light?" An unknown time of blessing followed, and the Lord performed wonders in that land.

Yet, notwithstanding this flourishing time, a problem continued to exist. The churches found their Lord but not one another. It is as bad as when churches find one another but do not find the Lord! "The wonders of God were attributed to the Holy Spirit by one group but to the devil by another group," said a Ugandan minister. The result was quarrels and divisions.

Idi Amin was able to exploit the differences between

some believers in Uganda. In late 1971 he discovered that all was not well among the top leaders of the Anglican Church of Uganda. One diocese was threatening to secede, and another was refusing to hold further discussions on the constitution. He decided to intervene and summoned all the bishops and diocesan councils to a meeting in the Conference Center in Kampala to straighten it out.

"I don't want a divided church in my country," he explained.

For two days the leaders sat and stared sullenly at one another, and the differences remained as wide as ever. But on November 28, the Lord gave the assembled group a message from Philippians. They saw that they were men "going up," each thinking about his own reputation and demanding his rights. But that day they caught a vision of the Man "coming down": Jesus, "Who, being in the form of God ... made himself of no reputation, and took upon him the form of a servant, and was made in the likeness of men: And ... he humbled himself ... even (to the death of the cross" (Philippians 2:6-8 KJV).

What a change Jesus made! "In His presence, our dear archbishop, the Most Reverend Erica Sabiti, and each of the nine diocesan bishops, went down in confession of the sins which had contributed to the divisions in the church, and a great melting by the Holy Spirit came upon us all," recalled Bishop Festo Kivengere, the Bishop of Kigezi.

President Amin often reminded the leaders that he had personally "saved the church!" although the believers knew that Jesus had done that. But sadly that episode showed to the Muslim dictator that the Christian Church in Uganda had weaknesses — fundamental weaknesses.

Discord always results in hatred, jealousy and criticism; the power of the Holy Spirit is lost. The consequences of Idi Amin's reign of terror had another effect. Although the godless authorities persecuted Christians, not only was there suffering and affliction but also blessing and victory. Believers found one another in unity and love, and the Holy Spirit once again became the Comforter of all. The Church became more prayerful and evangelism flourished.

When there was division among the churches, they were so busy with their own problems that they quite forgot there was a world outside of Uganda which needed the Gospel. But because of the persecution brought about by Idi Amin, church leaders had to flee, and they went into the world preaching the Gospel of love and forgiveness.

On my third visit to Uganda, a Ugandan church leader who lived in exile in Kenya accompanied me. He is a good friend of mine and is now affiliated with Open Doors. Although an Anglican, he took me to a Pentecostal church. The meeting between Anglican and Pentecostal Christians warmed my heart. There was joy as they greeted one another. "Idi Amin's persecution has brought us together," he explained.

If unity is not our aim now, then the Lord will send persecution. God does not lay burdens on us in order to break us, but to bring us to our knees. If we don't want to bend, then He will allow oppression to increase — until we find Him and one another.

## Upheaval in the Church

Rituals and different forms of worship can blind and bind us. A person who would shout "hallelujah" in some churches would certainly be put out of others. This actually happened in a village in Holland. The church was packed to capacity. It was the custom for the service to follow a fixed pattern: first a psalm, then a hymn, the Ten Commandments, a short prayer, a sermon of approximately twenty minutes, another hymn and a closing prayer — and, of course, the collection.

But this Sunday was different. The liturgy remained the same, but not the minister. He had chosen a few beautiful hymns and his sermon was full of fire. The congregation was not used to this type of preaching and as a result listened attentively. Even the children pricked up their ears. It was quite revolutionary, but it was not this that disturbed the church council.

The upheaval occurred shortly after the minister pronounced his "Amen." A man got up in the middle of the

church, looked at the minister and suddenly shouted,
"Hallelujah!" Consternation followed. Everyone looked
indignantly at the man. What was wrong with the fellow
to upset the service so?

The man looked about him in amazement. "Did I say
something wrong?" he seemed to be saying. He was just
about to sit down when two elders leapt out of their pews.
Taking great strides towards the "hallelujah" brother,
they pulled him out of his pew and took him into the
vestry.

The minister showed no reaction at all. He pronounced
his benediction and followed the elders into the vestry.
The poor brother was reprimanded; there was not much
the minister could do about it.

That morning everyone discussed the upheaval. They
soon forgot the sermon but not the upheaval.


## Look Farther Than Your Own Church

There is not much hope for a church when such a trivial
incident can bring about an upheaval. All that remains is
a legalistic form of religion without any life. If a spontaneous shout of joyful faith is quickly stifled, then we have
wandered far from the biblical pattern. We must learn to
regain the spontaneous faith in our churches — not in a
disorderly manner but according to the Bible.

It is even worse when a good biblical message is regarded as a danger. A preacher is often persecuted and
expelled if he does not keep to the letter of the church
law. Discord arises as soon as the gifts of the Spirit are
preached. How much evangelizing — or missionary work
— is judged because it does not originate from "our"
church! Instead of being thankful for the wonderful work
done by many interdenominational organizations, we
promote opposition and criticism.

We need to see further than our own church and be concerned about the Kingdom of God. We must give each
other the hand of fellowship instead of fighting against
one another. Instead of persecuting one another, we
should be fighting our mutual enemy, the powers of dark-

ness.

We have to learn to prepare ourselves for persecution through "unlearning" to persecute one another. Then only do we have hope — for the Church and for our nation. "But in humility count others better than yourselves. Let each of you look not only to his own interests, but also to the interests of others" (Philippians 2:3,4).

Chapter 8

## POINTS FOR PERSONAL REFLECTION

1. We are warned that some of the problems Christians face will come from those who are also identified as Christians. Note such warnings in Matthew 24:10 and Acts 20:29,30. Paul deals with an incipient problem of this sort in 1 Corinthians 1:10-12; 3:3-4.

2. Spiritual problems do not always lead to persecution of Christian by Christian, but they still can cause severe problems. Note the result in Acts 15:36-40. How do such disagreements, whoever may have been right, relate to Jesus' prayer for His church and the world in John 17:20-23?

3. Paul was a man of great zeal; he could be rather blunt at times in his dealings with others. But late in life he wrote a beautiful appeal and description of practical Christian unity in Philippians 2:18. Study this passage carefully and apply it to your life relationships.

**Chapter 9**

# THE CHURCH THAT CANNOT BE DESTROYED

Throughout the ages attempts have been made to destroy the Church of Jesus Christ. The battle is not in the first place directed at the Christian but at Christ Himself. "Why do you persecute me?" (Acts 9:4).

This battle began when Satan tried to usurp the position of God. Satan was still an angel of God. He could not bear it that God was superior to him and therefore endeavored to attack the throne of God. It was in vain; God punished him and threw him down to earth.

Then Satan began his second attack. The first one failed, the second would succeed. The attack on the throne of God ended in fiasco, but the attack on the throne in the hearts of men succeeded: Adam and Eve listened to him. They wanted, just as the devil wanted, to be like God. The consequence was the fall of man. Since then Satan has ruled over man.

Finally, Jesus Christ had to give His own life to set us free. From His birth to His death, He was in continuous battle with the father of sin. The attack Satan made on Jesus in the desert was more intense than we can ever imagine. Everything was directed toward getting Jesus to disobey God. The last temptation was the climax. The devil showed Jesus all the kingdoms of the world. "All these I will give you, if you will fall down and worship me" (Matthew 4:9).

It was a crafty trick of Satan. He knew that Jesus came to reconcile man with God, and seemed to be suggesting an easy solution. It was as though he had said, "Then You need not die on the cross. I will give you everything you expect to obtain by your death. I am making it easy. Acknowledge me and I will surrender everything over which I rule."

But Jesus saw right through the devil's suggestion; He knew that obedience to Satan meant disobedience to the Father. Instead of getting "all the kingdoms" from the devil, he would become his slave.

Later, when Jesus hung on the cross, Satan tried for the last time. Out of the mouths of the chief priests and scribes he called out: "Come down from the cross and we will believe." Jesus saw through their cunning and remained silent. Of course He could come down from the cross. He could order the angels to rescue Him. The deed would, however, mean disobedience to God. In this way Christ fought, until His death, against the prince of darkness, eventually to conquer him on the cross. "He disarmed the principalities and powers and made a public example of them, triumphing over them in him" (Colossians 2:15).

## The Battle Is Not Over

Satan is a conquered foe, but he still has not given up the battle. He knows his time is short, and therefore tries to bring as many people to a fall as possible. That is why he uses all types of weapons. His greatest concern is for the "unreached people." He realizes that he has to hand over many people (Christians) to his opponent, Jesus Christ. If the Christians obey the commission of God and spread the gospel to all nations, then he will lose even more people. That is why he tries to rock the Church of Christ to sleep, so that the "unreached people" will remain unreached. Or he blinds our eyes so that we are concerned only about our own church instead of the whole world. Another tactic is to encourage discord among Christians so that they will fight one another instead of the devil.

Satan also makes use of the *false prophet* — Mohammed — to keep people away from Christ. ("Allah is God and Mohammed is his prophet.") He uses *other religions*, such as Hinduism, Buddhism, etc., so that people will believe in "saving themselves" instead of accepting redemption through Christ. He infiltrates *capitalism*, which allows man to think he does not need God; Mammon takes the place of God.

Wealth can be a blessing, but it is also a curse. This was proved to me when I had a conversation with a rich businessman about Christ. I told him that he should seek the Kingdom of God and His righteousness, and that all the other things would be given to him. The man looked at me disdainfully and replied, "But I *have* all the 'other things' already. Why should I seek after God?" His possessions took the place of God.

The devil also uses *Communism* to persecute the Church of Christ and, if possible, to wipe it out. Karl Marx wanted to destroy God in whose existence he did not believe. How can one destroy someone who does not exist? It reminds me of a contradictory statement made by another atheist. This man was listening to an evangelist proclaiming the gospel on a street corner. The atheist started to argue with the preacher and maintained that there was no God. To substantiate his argument he claimed that three generations in his family were atheists. "My father was an atheist, I am an atheist and my son is, *thank God*, also an atheist!"

## The Humor of God

The French writer Voltaire (1694-1778) was filled with an intense hatred for Christians. "Destroy the Church," he called out, and followed his cry by writing a book in which he made a sharp attack on Christians. He compared the Church to a sinking ship with no chances of survival. "He who sits in the heavens laughs; the Lord has them in derision" (Psalm 2:4). He is not frightened by philosophers such as Voltaire. Voltaire is dead, but God is still on the throne. Voltaire's book is no longer read, but God's Word is still a best seller. Voltaire's house, where he wrote his atheistic hypotheses, is now being used by the French Bible Society as a Bible bookshop.

Such is the humor of God.

The Church isn't a sinking ship. Just as Noah's ark sur-

vived the flood, so will the Church of Jesus Christ with-
stand the storms of persecution during the end times.
Although there will be a great falling away, the future of
the Church of God is secure. "... And on this rock I will
build my church, and the powers of death shall not prevail
against it" (Matthew 16:18).

Despite all the pessimistic opinions regarding the
future of the Church of Christ, we receive optimism from
the Lord of the Church. He builds His Church and keeps
His Church. No devil, Nero, Voltaire, Idi Amin, Stalin or
Mao could ever change this. The Church of Christ may
form a minority in the future, but always a victorious
minority.

"The Church is in a bad state," someone will say and on
the basis of statistics show how it is losing ground, in
numbers as well as in influence. I see it differently. It is
going well with the Church, for reliable reports demonstrate that the Church has never grown as quickly as it is
growing today. Statistics from mission societies show
that an average of fifteen people per minute around the
world are committing their lives to Jesus Christ.

The Bible declares that there is great joy in heaven
when one sinner is saved. Now I can understand why the
angels always rejoice in the presence of God. Every time
someone is saved, they take up their harps and praise
God. They have scarcely finished the first line when the
next person is saved — fifteen every 60 seconds. For this
reason there is always joy in heaven! Martin Luther's
inspiring hymn, written over 400 years ago, says it all:


"A mighty fortress is our God,
A bulwark never failing,
Our helper He, amid the flood
Of mortal ills prevailing;
For still our ancient foe
Doth seek to work us woe;
His craft and pow'r are great,
And, armed with cruel hate,
On earth is not his equal."

No matter how great the attack, the Church of Christ cannot be destroyed. This is borne out by the revival that has swept through persecuted countries like Uganda and China. This does not concern a specific denomination, but the universal Church of God. Should things become more difficult in the future, the Church never has to bow its head or become discouraged. "So we do not lose heart ... For this slight momentary affliction is preparing for us an eternal weight of glory beyond all comparison, because we look not to the things that are seen but to the things that are unseen; for the things that are seen are transient, but the things that are unseen are eternal" (2 Corinthians 4:16-18).

Nor can the throne of God be destroyed. "Thy throne, O God, is for ever and ever ..." (Hebrews 1:8). No one can dethrone God.

The Word of God cannot be destroyed: "The word of the Lord abides for ever" (1 Peter 1:25).

This is the Church's consolation. The throne of God, the Church of Jesus Christ and the Word of God will abide until eternity.

## Our Problems — God's Plans

God never has problems. He only has plans. That is why there is no panic in heaven.

Brother Andrew's great friend, Corrie ten Boom, uses the illustration of a tapestry. If you look at the wrong side you see a confusion of threads. You are unable to make out a pattern. Our lives are often like this. If you just see the problems, you ask yourself if anything can ever come out of it.

This was the experience of Elisha's servant. When the city was surrounded by the enemy, he could see no way out and so he shouted, "Alas, my master! What shall we do?" He could see only the problem and was at the end of his wits. Elisha encouraged him: "Fear not, for those who are with us are more than those who are with them" (2 Kings 6:16). A strange answer! Yet Elisha was right. The servant's problem was that he only saw the enemy

and was totally blinded to spiritual realities. "Then
Elisha prayed, and said, 'O Lord, I pray thee, open his
eyes that he may see.' So the Lord opened the eyes of the
young man, and he saw; and behold, the mountain was full
of horses and chariots of fire round about Elisha" (verse
17).

With our natural eyes we can only see our problems,
but if our spiritual eyes are opened, then we see the glory
and plan of God.

David also experienced this when he heard Goliath
ranting and raving. The Israelites were afraid of the
giant. "He is so big, we cannot defeat him," was their
human reaction. David looked at Goliath through
spiritual eyes and said, "He is so big, I cannot *miss* him!"
Then he picked up a few stones, put one in his sling and
slung it, striking the Philistine on the forehead. Goliath
fell, stunned.

The Israelites' problem was David's plan: " . . . that all
the earth may know that there is a God in Israel, and that
all this assembly may know that the Lord saves not with
sword and spear; for the battle is the Lord's and he will
give you into our hand" (1 Samuel 17:46-47).

I recently visited Laos again. It is now a Communist
country, and I was afraid the Communists would recognize me. While still in the plane I prayed and confessed
my fear to the Lord. It was if the Lord said to me, "Do not
fear. Trust in Me." This gave me peace.

When we were above the Vientiane airport we were advised that we could not land immediately. There were
thousands of Communist soldiers on the airfield, busy
with an exercise and using the only landing strip available. We circled the airfield several times while the pilot
remained in contact with the control tower. Finally the
landing strip was cleared, and the Communist soldiers
stood on either side of the airstrip as we came in. I looked
through the window and felt the same as Elisha's servant.
"O Lord, what now?" Then God opened my eyes. "You are
not seeing right. Look at the people as I see them." It
changed everything. I looked again and saw — the Communists were like tiny grasshoppers!

That is the secret: the higher you are, the smaller the

people. It is the same from a spiritual point of view. The problems become smaller as we take up our position in Christ. He "made us sit with him in the heavenly places" (Ephesians 2:6). Things look different from there. Then our problems change into plans.

The Church in Communist countries has the same witness. The persecution of Christians in Russia and China did not result in defeat but in victory! The chaff is separated from the kernel as a result of the falling away of nominal Christians. The churches in China were closed, yet the numbers of Christians increased.

The Communist ideology may overflow into many countries, religious freedom may disappear, but the Church of Jesus Christ still stands and grows. For this reason we can meet the future with the fullest confidence, not because of our great faith, but because of the faithfulness of our great God. He keeps the church in His hand.

Martin Luther's hymn continues:

"Did we in our own strength confide,
Our striving would be losing,
Were not the right Man on our side,
The Man of God's own choosing.
Dost ask who that may be?
Christ Jesus, it is He;
Lord Sabaoth His name,
From age to age the same,
And He must win the battle."

His Throne, His Word and His Church stand. Does it mean that we can sit back in our easy chairs and take a spiritual forty winks? Definitely not! God, who sits on the throne and builds His Church, wants us to become actively involved in His Kingdom — not as spectators but as participants.

Chapter 9

## POINTS FOR PERSONAL REFLECTION

1. The Church of Jesus Christ can never be destroyed because it is built upon sure foundations. Consider the

statements in Matthew 16:18, Hebrews 1:8; and 1 Peter 1:23-25.

2. God's authority over the nations and history is beautifully expressed in Psalm 2:1-6. Read it prayerfully and note its ending: "Happy are all who find refuge in Him!" How does this apply to your life?

3. When we find ourselves in the midst of trouble and persecution, we need the assurance of God's Word and a knowledge of His will. Do you find this assurance in Paul's description of the activity of the Trinity on our behalf in Romans 8:26-39?

# Chapter 10

# SPECTATORS OR PARTICIPANTS?

Once on a tour through Russia and Siberia I met many fanatical Communists. The impression I received was that they were totally dedicated to their ideology.

When I spoke to one of them about the Gospel, he laughed. "If you really believe Jesus is your Savior, why don't you win the world for Him? We Communists really believe in our ideology, and in the sixty years we've been in existence we have already won half the world. A few more years and the whole world will be at our feet."

Then he said something which made my flesh crawl: "Shall I tell you what the difference is between us? You Christians are spectators, and we Communists are participants."

He was right; in the Christian world we have many spectators and few participants. This is our big problem.

It reminds me of a soccer match. If you listen to the shouting and whistling of the crowds, you wonder where the best players are, in the stands or on the field? It would appear that the spectators know the rules better than the players or referee. Yet they remain shouting spectators and do not become involved. Should you put them on the field you would see that they could not do much with their two left feet. But they are able to shout!

We have a lot of these spectators in our churches. They can tell you exactly what is wrong with the work in the church. The elder doesn't do enough visitation, the minister does not preach well, the only visit they receive is from the deacon who comes to collect the money, etc., etc. These spectators know it all, but they don't want to get involved. Should you make any demand upon them, they turn out to be spectators only, criticizing without getting involved.

The Lord wants us to be involved in His Kingdom. God's Church is not a pleasure launch but a cargo boat. There is no place for passengers, only a crew.

The great English missionary, C. T. Studd, put it so well: "Let us not glide through this world and then slip quietly into heaven, without having blown the trumpet loud and long for our Redeemer, Jesus Christ. Let us see to it that the devil will hold a thanksgiving service in hell when he gets the news of our departure from the field of battle."

We need to be participants, witnesses of the salvation of Christ, to give the devil a nervous breakdown because of our continued witnessing. The reaction of Satan when we die should be, luckily, one less witness for Jesus.

Those who are spectators now will be the first to fall away during times of persecution. "Whoever denies me before men, I also will deny before my Father who is in heaven" (Matthew 10:33). If we are ashamed of Him, He will be ashamed of us.

The opposite is also true. "So every one who acknowledges me before men, I also will acknowledge before my Father who is in heaven" (Matthew 10:32).

## Dedication to the Revolution

Mao's little Red Book of quotations was found on the body of a dead soldier in Zimbabwe. He had received it from a Chinese advisor and had obviously studied it thoroughly. On leafing through the book I found that the guerrilla had underlined many of Mao's statements. And on the first page he wrote something every Christian should write in his Bible: "Every sentence, every word of this book is true. It is a mighty weapon. Forward to victory, fear no sacrifice. One spark out of this book can cause a mighty fire."

That is the language of a dedicated guerrilla. No sacrifice is considered too great for his revolution. He was prepared to die for it, and he did. Many Christians would rather remain spectators; it is safer.

If we want to stop the Communist revolution, we will have to become involved in the Kingdom of God.

George Meany, the American trade union leader, once declared, "The conflict between communism and freedom is the greatest problem of our time. It overshadows all other problems. The future of the whole human race depends on the outcome of the conflict."

The Communists believe they will ultimately win, and they work toward their victory. They have one aim: to triumph. Incited with a burning dsire to win, no sacrifice is considered too great.

I firmly believe Communism will not be destroyed with weapons. It is an ideology which dominates millions of people. It rules with an iron hand over its subjects. Although only six percent of the Russians are members of the Communist Party, this small minority has dictatorial power over the remaining ninety-four percent.

The Communist state has replaced God. The aim of this ideology is to conquer the whole world. For this, no one and nothing will be spared. In each country they will try to get a selected part of the population on their side, making all kinds of promises. It is a tactic which was propagated by the then Chinese premier, Chou En-lai, many years ago. He said, "If you want to detroy someone but you are unable to get near him, then you must befriend him. Once you are his friend, you can embrace him and stick a knife in his back."

That method is still being practiced today. A friendship is formed with a certain number of people, not because they particularly love them or want to help them but to use them for their own purposes. As soon as the Communists have the power in hand, they turn against their former allies. Overnight their friends become enemies.

There is only *one* way of breaking the Communist power: "And this is the victory that overcomes the world, our faith" (1 John 5:4). Our faith in Jesus Christ, as the Redeemer of the world, and our dedication to Him must be greater than the dedication of the Communists to their ideology. We must regain that living, vibrant faith if we are to endure the battle against an enemy who plans to destroy us.

Let socialism give Christ a chance, give Him a free hand to manifest His revolutionary and character-transforming power. Christ will carry through the most profound, wholesome revolution in this society. The Christ Revolution will meet the need of the socialist society.

Men who seek to transform the whole world need only fear Christ because He points out that this transformation must first begin with the individual, in his own character. Revolution must start with ourselves and only He who loved mankind so much that He was prepared to be crucified for them can do this. Socialism needs the sacrificial spirit of Christ. Will it take up this offer? This is the major question to which we await an answer.

Communism forms an enormous challenge to Christianity. Although I am against Communism, I am more concerned about the lack of zeal of Christians than I am about the zeal of the Communists. The Communists will never win the battle unless the Christians remain spectators.

## Guerrilla for Christ

One young Christian who was forced to leave the grandstand to get involved in the spiritual battle was Salu Daka Ndebele, a black Zimbabwean.

On May 5, 1973, Salu, who was from the township of Mpopoma in Bulawayo, Zimbabwe, accepted the Lord Jesus Christ into his life as his own personal Savior. Like many Christians, he felt he would now have a life of peace and joy — the soft Gospel that many preachers offer.

After a period of training with Youth with a Mission, Salu moved to Maputo as part of a multi-racial team, to work with the capital's drug addicts. The whole time he was in the city, Salu could feel the undercurrent of tension. Then the Portuguese Government announced they were handing over the government to the Marxist Front for the Liberation of Mozambique.

In July, 1975, Salu and many of the missionaries were imprisoned in Polana Prison, where they were shocked by the disgusting, inhuman conditions, torture, harassment, cold-blooded executions, and the horrible practice of homosexuals, drunks and gamblers.

But then he was faced with a difficult decision: to be-

come a guerrilla or die in jail. In the stifling interrogation
room of the police headquarters, a police chief told him,
"Salu Daka, you can rot in prison for forty years until you
have changed your imperialist ideas." His captor, a plain-
clothes officer wearing a brown leather jacket, pointed to
the Soviet-made machine gun at his side and added, "We
want to kill your God. We want to give you a gun so you
can go and fight for Zimbabwe against the racist Ian
Smith. But if you won't fight, you will stay in jail forever."

Salu's mind was in a daze as this callous man in his
thirties stared at him with steel-cold eyes and tried to
tear his two-year-old faith in Jesus Christ to shreds. He
shook in fright as the verbal bombardment went on. "We
are going to wipe out all your imperialist ideas about religion," he yelled at Salu with a clipped, machine-gun deliv-
ery. "If you do not change your ideas, you are going to
prison for a long time."

The policeman looked startled as Salu summoned up
enough courage to wipe the beads of perspiration from
his knotted brow and say, with a voice that was almost
cracking, "Praise God! Then I will go to prison, and I'll
stay there for forty years if necessary. God will be with
me, and I will never change my mind about Him. I will
never deny Him."

That was not an easy thing for this young believer to
say. All he had to do was to say he would become a guerrilla to fight Ian Smith, and he would immediately be released.

He chose instead to be a GUERRILLA FOR CHRIST.
For sixteen terrible months he suffered agonies for his
faith in that prison, but finally he was released. Where
did he go then? To war-torn Northern Ireland to work as
an evangelist there. Salu believes Christians should be in
the front-line — not in the stands watching. But there's a
price to pay, as he can testify.

## Love Instead of Hate

In the seething township of Soweto, on the edge of Johannesburg, South Africa, where more than a million

black people live, resides the Dube family. Benjamin Dube was an evangelist who witnessed on Soweto streets of his faith in Jesus Christ. His message was that instead of hating one another, blacks must love whites and whites must love blacks. He was threatened many times. One day some black people approached him and commanded him not to preach about loving one another any more. "We do not want to love our neighbor, but to hate him," they told evangelist Dube.

Benjamin carried on regardlessly. One night he dreamed he was stabbed to death by his own people. He awoke and woke up his wife, Grace. "I believe this dream is going to happen," he said. "We will have to decide: Carry on and suffer, or stop and, in so doing, disobey God."

The following day they discussed the dream and also the constant threat with their children. "Must I continue this message of forgiveness?" Benjamin asked his children. All four nodded, although they were well aware of the consequences.

Benjamin Dube prayed together with his wife and children, asking the Lord for strength to remain faithful. Not long afterward, evangelist Dube had to preach at a meeting again. His children were with him. In the middle of Soweto his car was stopped by ten black men. They dragged the faithful preacher out of the car and stabbed a knife into his chest sixteen times. The children fled; twelve-year-old Bonani hid behind a dustbin. He saw how his father was stabbed again and again, but he knew he was unable to help.

The murderers took Benjamin's Bible and dipped it into his blood, then they disappeared into a dark street. Little Bonani ran to his father, but he was dead. Bonani then ran home and told his mother the horrible news. Immediately he went to his bedroom and in his great need and sorrow called out to God. He picked up the Bible lying next to his bed and opened it. The first words he read were the words of Jesus on the cross: "Father, forgive them, for they know not what they do."

Later the murderers were arrested. Seven of the ten were sentenced to three months' imprisonment because they had only helped to plan the murder, but were not directly involved. The others were given fifteen years.

After the funeral, Grace and her children got together and decided they would not refrain from their message of love and forgiveness. Together with her children she still witnesses in word and song about the redemption of Christ.

About a year after the death of her husband, Grace and her children were holding an open-air meeting. The seven accomplices were on the loose again. After Grace and her children had sung a song, she gave her testimony. She ended with a call to repentance: "Friends, begin a new life with Jesus. He takes away all hate and gives love in return. Come and talk to me if you want to follow Jesus."

There was a movement in the crowd. Young and old came forward. Suddenly a man pushed through and stood with head bowed before Grace Dube. "I also want to start a new life with Jesus," he said softly.

Grace looked at the young man and trembled. The man was one of the seven accomplices who had planned the murder of her husband. He did not look at her, and for a moment Grace did not know what to say. Then she put her arms around him and, through tears, told him, "Now you are my brother."

A deathly silence descended on the crowd. They had recognized the man, too, and so had Grace's children. While everyone looked on, the children began to sing, "What a mighty God we serve, let us praise and glorify Him!"

Benjamin Dube didn't want to be a looker-on; neither did his wife and family. They would rather be participants and die than spectators and live. "And they have conquered him by the blood of the Lamb and by the word of their testimony, for they loved not their lives even unto death" (Revelation 12:11).

## The Bible's Freedom Fighters

Benjamin Dube was a freedom fighter. He preached deliverance from sin through faith in Christ Jesus.

Many Western churches today proclaim that Chris-

tians cannot remain spectators but must become participants. Their way of becoming involved is by giving practical support to the so-called "liberation movement." This
does not involve the preaching of the gospel but the over-
throwing of political institutions by violence. Collections
are taken up in many churches for these political causes.
They maintain that the funds are used to buy food and
medicine, not weapons.

This is not a true presentation of affairs, however.
Indirectly, the so-called liberation movements are aided
in this way to wage war. In Laos I saw how funds, meant
for purchasing medicine, were used to buy weapons. I was
invited to attend the handing over of the medicine. Displayed in an open field were weapons.

The commanding officer's speech answered my questions. "We should have used the money to buy medicine,"
he began. "Because medicine is used to treat war victims,
we have decided to use the money in a different way. The
quickest method to finish off a war is to buy more
weapons and destroy the enemy. There will be a short
time in which victims will perish, but then the war will be
over. That is why we have used the money to buy the necessary weapons." A long applause followed. A heathen
witch doctor was then asked to dedicate the weapons to
their forefathers and to have them blessed.

The Bible does not support such practices. Christ did
not revolt against the existing Roman rule. Although His
ministry occurred at the time of Roman control, Jesus
never preached violence. He proclaimed another Kingdom which was not of this world. Rather than take up the
sword against Pilate, he went to Pilate and received the
Cross.

Nowadays, the proclaiming of the Gospel is often
connected with political structures and opinions. Much
missionary work is substituted by the supporting of "liberation movements." Those missionaries are no longer
concerned with the forgiveness of sins but with the re-
jecting of specific governments, if need be, with violence.

The apostles were sent into a hostile world. They lived
in an occupied area. The Roman government had all the

power. What was the commission given to the apostles? To create unrest among the people in the hope that the Romans would be driven out? Did they support the liberation movements of that time (think about the Zealots) and take up collections in the churches? No! The order was clear: They had to witness about the forgiveness of sins through Jesus Christ "... in Jerusalem and in all Judea and Samaria and to the end of the earth" (Acts 1:18).

Samaria was also an inaccessible area for the disciples, "for Jews have no dealings with Samaritans" (John 4:9). Earlier the disciples themselves had behaved as true "liberators." They wanted to destroy the Samaritans (Luke 9:54).

After Philip's successful evangelization of Samaria, Peter and John went up to pray for the Samaritans to receive the Holy Spirit. Prayer was the answer, instead of weapons (Acts 8:15). The Holy Spirit came in all His fullness, and enmity was changed into brotherly love. Times have changed, but the command remains the same: "Go therefore and make disciples of all nations" (Matthew 28:19).

Everyone who obeys Christ's commandment belongs to His liberation movement.

## To Divide Is to Multiply

If a nation is threatened, there is the danger of seeing only its own problems. And the more it looks at those problems, the bigger the problems become. A threatened country receives greater blessing if it looks beyond its own problems.

The best form of defense is still attack. This applies in the spiritual realm as well. We cannot sit back and bemoan our lot; we must look forward and push forward.

There is a law which exists in the Kingdom of God but is unknown to the world. That law is simply: "To divide is to multiply." When Jesus fed the crowd of five thousand, He had only five loaves of bread and two fish. He did not complain about the impossible situation; neither did He send the crowds home. No, He gave the disciples instructions to distribute the food to the crowd. They looked at Him in bewilderment: "We have only five loaves here and two fish" (Matthew 14:17).

"Bring them here," Jesus said. He blessed them and began to break the bread. Then the miracle happened! The more they broke off and shared, the more they received. Finally, all five thousand men were fed, as well as the women and children. And there was still bread left over.

Paradoxically, in the Christian life, to divide is to multiply. The person who has little but dares to give it to Jesus, will quickly see the wonders Jesus is able to perform with it.

"One man gives freely, yet grows all the richer; another withholds what he should give, and only suffers want. A liberal man will be enriched, and one who waters will himself be watered" (Proverbs 11:24-25).

## A Missionary Diet

To be involved with the Kingdom of God is the best way to prepare yourself for a time of need. Brother Andrew puts it this way: "God will save the country in which He sees enough potential for world evangelism." I do believe that many Western countries have enough potential, but more people need to become involved with the work of God and not remain spectators. "Lift up your eyes, and see how the fields are already white for harvest" (John 4:35).

The world must be reached with the message of the Gospel. This is harvest time; we cannot permit ourselves to be forever busy with our own problems, for "a son who sleeps in harvest brings shame" (Proverbs 10:5). This is why we should reach beyond the borders of our own church and country.

John Wesley said, "The world is my parish." Unfortunately, today too many ministers switch this around: "My parish is my world." They do not see beyond their own churches. They say, "There is so much to be done in my own church that it is impossible to think about missionary work."

Yes, if we only see our own church, there will always be

plenty to do. Christ gave the order that the Gospel must be preached to the whole creation. Yet, there are more people today who have not been reached than there ever were before. More and more countries are closing their doors to missionary work. I have mentioned the reason: Communism is so active; it is taking over country after country. If Christians, however, wake up, and if ministers regain the missionary vision and obey it, only then will we be able to bring a halt to Communism.

Why do we have to minister to the same people Sunday after Sunday without becoming involved with missionary work? If we do not activate the Church, but only keep preaching to the same people every Sunday, they do not become more spiritual but only fatter — so fat that God cannot get them into action anymore.

A fat church is a sick church. The best medicine for a sick church is to put them on a missionary diet! The more we share, the more we will receive — in the spiritual as well as in the financial aspect. A church which is alive is a church doing missionary work. And a mission-oriented church is a financially sound church.

## The Back Rows

I want to refer to the feeding of the five thousand again, using an illustration used by Dr. Oswald Smith, founder of the People's Church in Toronto, Canada. The people had to sit in rows. Then what happened? We might imagine that the disciples each had a basket with bread, and they served the first rows. At the end of the first row they waited until all the people had eaten their bread; then they offered them a second piece, and a third and a fourth. When the first row had eaten enough, they went to the second row; and when they had eaten enough, they went to the third row. . . .

No, it didn't happen that way. It would not have been right! The people in the back rows would have protested: "Here. Come here. Give us something too. We also are hungry. Why do you give the people in the front rows so much and so often, while we get nothing?"

There are those "back rows" today, people who are

hungry, not only physically but also spiritually. They have never had the opportunity to hear the Gospel because we concentrate on the first row. They have been waiting for almost two thousand years. The people in the front row are hearing about Jesus' Second Coming while the back rows have never even heard about His First Coming!

In 1971, on the island of Guam in the Pacific Ocean, people discovered a Japanese man who had been sent there in 1942. This man lived in isolation, deep in the jungle, still under the impression that there was a war. The good news that the war had been over for twenty-five years never reached him. Eventually, in 1972, he was found and heard the news of his life. How is it possible that this could take place in our modern world?

My thoughts go back to the back rows. I ask again: How is it possible that there are still thousands of towns where people have not had the opportunity of hearing the Good News that Jesus brought peace almost two thousand years ago by dying on the cross, the "expiation for our sins, and not for ours only but also for the sins of the whole world" (1 John 2:2).

A few years ago people from a tribe in a remote part of Laos came in contact with the Gospel for the first time. I was the first missionary to work with this tribe. When one of the inhabitants came to repentance, he said, "Now we can tell our children for the first time that Jesus also loves us."

That is why we have to go. We must become involved in the Kingdom of God. It *can* still happen. The night is coming when no one can work. It is getting more difficult; more countries are closing their doors. It seems as though missionary work has been written off in those countries — but not by God. He wants to reach the world — through us. There are still many countries to which we can go. "Go therefore." We can only pray, "Father, forgive us, because we don't know what we have refused to do."

## Where Are the Men?

It is sad to see that there are four times as many

women in the mission field as men. I have met some of
them in little remote villages in the mountains. I had to
walk for hours to get to their mission stations. They had
given up all and were prepared to live in loneliness. There
was no thought of a private life. Many of them do a man's
job.

When I think of the many vacancies at mission stations,
I feel guilty. Where are the young men in our country
who could take on these positions? What will induce a
man to take on such a post, now taken on by women? Is
the Lord's instruction not enough, or the need of people,
or the short time we have available? Fortunately, there
are still many who go, some of them under the most difficult circumstances.

I think of a young man who went to France to do
evangelistic work. He had a heart problem and had been
treated many times by the famed South African heart
specialist, Prof. Christiaan Barnard. As far as his health
was concerned, he should not have gone, but his love for
the Lord and for the people of France was greater than
his concern over his health.

Although he was extremely weak, he left for France
and began to learn their language. After a few months he
had another heart attack and died. On the back of the
door in his room they found a piece of paper on which was
written, "I am learning French for Jesus."

It is touching that his love for the Lord was so great
that he was prepared to bring his greatest offering — his
own life. His place is empty now. Where are the healthy
young men to take his place?

On a visit to friends in Vietnam we rode in a Jeep to an
isolated village. The way seemed impassable. There had
been a heavy downpour, and the sand road resembled a
quagmire instead of a road. We continually got stuck; the
wheels made deep tracks in the mud. Halfway, we felt
like giving up. The road went through a forest, and it
would have taken us at least another hour before we
would arrive at the village. There wasn't a person or
house in sight, and because of the war it appeared to be
safer to return home. That, however, was not feasible.
While we could hardly move forward, it would have been

practically impossible to turn around. We decided to try once more.

At a curve in the road we saw a young boy pushing his bicycle. He was walking ankle-deep in mud and was pushing his bicycle with difficulty. On the back of the bike was an icebox containing ice cream. The boy was going to the same village we were. He had been on the road for many hours and was only halfway. Yet he smiled when we chatted with him. Yes, he considered it worth his while, because he wanted to earn a few cents.

He actually was willing to walk through the mud, because he had something to sell. We, who were taking the Gospel to the next village, found the road too difficult and wanted to turn back!

We can learn much from the world — from the Russians and the Chinese, the Cubans and this Vietnamese boy. We can learn from the Dubes, from the missionary women and from the heart patient. We will have to make a decision: to be a spectator or a participant.

Chapter 10

## POINTS FOR PERSONAL REFLECTION

1. Jesus gave his disciples a final command, the Great Commission, just before He went back to heaven. Trace it in all its forms: Matthew 28:18-20; Mark 16:15; Luke 24:46-49; John 20:21; Acts 1:8.

2. That command is still valid: Jesus indicates this in Matthew 24:14. Paul showed he understood its application to him immediately after his conversion, Acts 9:20-22; he was sure that the Great Commission and its promises applied to him right to the end of his ministry, 2 Timothy 4:17-18. How does it apply to us?

3. It seems God leaves little room for us to be just spectators in the spiritual warfare around us. Consider the commission given in Ezekiel 33:7-9.

4. We all want to be overcomers. The secret of victory and being an overcomer is found in 1 John 5:4 and Revelation 12:11. How do these apply to your life?

# A SPIRITUAL BATTLE: A SPIRITUAL VICTORY

In 1944 a Mexican Communist leader said the following: "To hope for a Communist victory is useless if we do not stamp out Christianity." The Communists are very outspoken about Christianity.

Anatole Lunarsharsky, quoted earlier, said that Christian love is retarding the development of the Communist revolution. His slogan was: "We need hate; only then will we win the world." At the same time, Radio Leningrad went into action and continuously attacked Christians with a bombardment of verbal insults. "The Gospel and the Christian legends must be fought without sympathy and with all possible means," declared one announcer.

One of their most cunning methods is to infiltrate the Church and so destroy it. They try to influence ministers in the free West so that Communism will not be seen as a danger. Instead of taking up a position against the atheistic ideology, many Western churches are talking about having a dialogue with the Communists. Some ministers call themselves "Christian Marxists."

In the preceding chapter, I stated that I am fully convinced we cannot defeat Communism with weapons. We must be aware of the difference between Communism and Communists. Our battle is a spiritual one: "For we are not contending against flesh and blood, but against the principalities, against the powers, against the world rulers of this present darkness, against the spiritual hosts of wickedness in the heavenly places" (Ephesians 6:12).

Communism is more than just a political system. It is an ideology — or rather, a religion. Behind this "religion" are the powers of darkness. They are the real enemies of the Christian. They are also a conquered enemy because, on the cross, Christ triumphed over them (Colossians 2:15).

Because of this victory we can go to meet the enemy. Against the spiritual hosts of wickedness in heavenly places we have the power of the Holy Spirit. All the powers of darkness tremble in His presence. "For he who is in you is greater than he who is in the world" (1 John 4:4). Because the enemy is a spiritual enemy, only a spiritual victory is possible. "Behold, I have given you authority to tread upon serpents and scorpions, and over all the power of the enemy . . ." (Luke 10:19).

## The Secret of Victory

In Exodus 17:8-16 a spiritual battle is won over the Amalekites. The strategy and aggressiveness of Joshua was not a guarantee for victory. The actual battle was fought on the mountaintop where Moses stood. He did not stand with a rifle in his hand, but with the staff of God. He fought a spiritual battle: "Whenever Moses held up his hand, Israel prevailed; and whenever he lowered his hand, Amalek prevailed" (verse 11).

No matter how strong Joshua's army was, the victory was won on another front. Moses, Aaron and Hur battled in prayer. When Moses grew tired and could not hold up his hands, he needed two friends — praying partners — to help him.

"So his hands were steady until the going down of the sun. And Joshua mowed down Amalek and his people with the edge of the sword" (verses 12 and 13). "So" is the key word. It did not depend on Joshua's strategy. The victory came about because of continued prayer. "A hand upon the banner of the Lord!" (verse 16). Against this the armed force of Amalek could do nothing.

This principle still applies. Woe to us if we put our faith in human power and military forces. Although Joshua and his men were needed to wage the battle against flesh and blood (Amalek), Moses had to impress upon Joshua that the victory came from God. *Jehovah-nisi* — "the Lord is my banner" (verse 15).

This incident also teaches us that it was not necessary for Moses to go into the valley with Joshua in order to pray. He was able to pray at another place — on the mountaintop. Because we wage a spiritual battle, we gain the victory against the powers of darkness without being present at the earthly battle scene. We can pray from our home or our church for the people of God in Russia, China, Vietnam and Mozambique. We do not have to be at the particular place of persecution to be able to pray effectively. We can even call upon other Christians to lift up their hands with us to God on behalf of the Suffering Church. We can support one another's hands. We can divert the attack of the prince of darkness against the church of Jesus Christ; all we need is a prayer group of two or more people.

That is why, in our work at Open Doors, we attach so much value to the faithful prayer groups who pray for the Suffering Church. We keep our prayer partners informed of the battle; without them we know that we are unable to do our work. The teams which go out and do this dangerous work know that the victory is not won because of their dedication and strategy but because of the faithful intercessors on the home front.

Recently, when I had to make a dangerous trip into a Communist country, an elderly brother came to me and said, "I appreciate your courage. I cannot go with you. All I can do is pray for you." I told him that the success of my trip would depend on him and his intercession. "Thorough, enduring mission work is done on our knees." That is where the spiritual battle is fought, before the face of the living God.

The devil laughs at our striving and display of military power, but he trembles when he sees a Christian pray. Prayer remains our secret weapon.

## On the Waiting List

In 1976, Brother Andrew and I visited Uganda for the first time. We were invited by the Anglican Church of Uganda to see what we could do for the believers there. There was a great need and, after many discussions with church leaders, we decided to send in 50,000 Bibles.

It was a dangerous trip, but we knew we had many prayer groups who were one with us in the battle. Their intercession bore fruit as there was a tremendous victory. The day before our departure we went to the travel agency in Kampala to confirm our flight. Although our air tickets were in order, it appeared that our names were on a waiting list. We advised them that our return flight was booked in Kenya and that they could verify this via their computer. The lady just smiled and told us that there were no computers in Uganda. Our names were right at the bottom of the waiting list, with sixteen others above ours.

The problem was that our visas would expire the following day. If we could not board the plane in due time, the following day we would be in Uganda illegally. Friends told us it was probably a ruse of Idi Amin's government to get us into trouble; our names probably were put on the waiting list for that reason.

We went back to the hotel room and knelt before the Lord. We knew this was a spiritual battle. Idi Amin did not want to let us go. Our thoughts went to our prayer partners. "Lord, lay it upon their hearts to pray for us," we asked the Lord.

We also claimed His promise that He would bountifully supply all our needs. Were we not His ambassadors? Then we should be treated like ambassadors. The plane would be leaving at five that afternoon. We decided to go to the airport at Entebbe as early as possible to see if anything else could be done.

When we arrived we saw no one else except two passengers who also had decided to come early. They were standing at the counter where all luggage was to be weighed. A half hour later more passengers came and stood behind us. Soon the line became longer and longer. The lady who was to give us our seating tickets did not turn up. It was five o'clock and she still wasn't there. Fortunately, we could see the plane, ready for its departure.

At half past five the lady came, together with an Ugandan soldier. Standing behind the counter, he called out for silence. Immediately it was quiet. "Ladies and gentlemen, please listen carefully. I don't want you to panic. There is a problem. We do not know where the passenger list is. We will start in front. Those who came first will be helped first."

Brother Andrew and I were the first to enter the plane. I asked the stewardess where we could sit.

"Take any seat, sir," she said. "The plane is yours." That was true ambassador treatment! "Thank you, Lord — uh ... miss," I said and sank into the first and best seat.

Later on we heard how the Lord had laid it on the hearts of our prayer partners to pray for us. "I thought so much about you and knew you were in trouble," one sister told me.

That is the reality of a spiritual battle. Our prayer partners were not with us in Uganda, but they knew of our need. They prayed — and the passenger list disappeared.

## In Prison

The devil has no answer for the prayer of faith in a Christian. In times of persecution and need, prayer remains the mightiest weapon. Christians in Communist countries experience this daily. Georgi Vins, the unregistered Baptist Church leader who has been banished from the Soviet Union, testified to it on his arrival in the United States. "When the Communist guards, without reason, treated us better, we knew it was because of the prayers and intercession of our friends in the West," Vins said.

A Ugandan minister, Pastor Joshua Musoke, also testified to this. His congregation prayed continuously for him when he was arrested by the infamous State Research Bureau, men from Amin's Gestapo. The news of his arrest reached us on the same day. We immediately informed some prayer groups, which came together to intercede for him.

The Lord answered their prayers in a wonderful way. Pastor Joshua was taken to the notorious headquarters of the State Research Bureau at Nakasero in Kampala. Hundreds of people were killed in the most gruesome ways. Many were murdered with a sledgehammer by a fellow prisoner. They had to kneel and were hit repeatedly on the head until they died. Then that prisoner was killed in a similar way. The final man was then shot by a guard.

"Killing this way saves bullets," explained a State Research officer.

Musoke was locked up in this underground prison. He stood ankle-deep in water mixed with urine and the blood of former victims. The stench was unbearable. When the door closed behind him, he found himself alone in this dark hole. Fear gripped his heart, and in his desperate need he called out to the Lord: "O Lord, help me. I am not afraid to die, but I am afraid of the suffering. Let the soldiers come and kill me immediately, but let the suffering be short."

The Holy Spirit comforted him and reminded him of Paul and Silas in prison at Philippi. With tears still in his eyes he began to praise and glorify the Lord. His guards, standing outside the door, heard him and thought he had lost his mind. They opened the cell door and pulled him outside and took him to the prison commander. He stared at Musoke in surprise. "What is wrong with you?" he asked.

Musoke lifted his hands heavenward and again began to praise the Lord. "You can kill me if you want to," he told the commander, "but I will continue to praise the Lord." And this he kept on doing.

The commander looked at Musoke and shook his head. "Totally mad," he said. "Let him go so he can die at home."

A few minutes later Musoke stood outside, a free man. He ran home, where the Christians were still on their knees praying. When they saw him, they embraced him. Tears of joy flowed down their cheeks. Then they lifted up their hands and praised the Lord.

"There is real power in intercession and praise," the beaming Musoke told me later.

"The prayer of a righteous man has great power in its effects" (James 5:16). This power is always at our disposal, in times of need and in times of freedom. Prayer bridges distances — not only between God and us, but also between us and the Suffering Church.

## Murdered

Many Christians have not survived the ordeal of suffering and torture. Did they suffer defeat? No, there was victory despite their physical struggle and pain. Stories of martyrs from church history testify to this. A few years ago, two of my American missionary colleagues, Evelyn Armstrong and Bea Kosin, were murdered in Laos. Evelyn, a nurse, took care of me at the time I was in the Kengkok hospital with cerebral malaria.

A few weeks after my discharge from the hospital, in the spring of 1972, the North Vietnamese Communists attacked the town. The two lady missionaries who were with the Brethren Organization, Christian Missions in Many Lands, hid in a house for two days. Local believers brought them food, but eventually they were discovered by the Communists and bound with barbed wire, their backs against each other. Then they were locked up in a room where they were left for three days. Every movement brought acute pain. They received no food or water. Finally, as the government forces launched an offensive to retake Kengkok, the Vietnamese soldiers dragged them to open ground in the town, and announced the two young prisoners would have to die.

The barbed wire was removed from their bodies, and they fell exhausted to the ground. They knew they would be shot.

"Do you have a last request?" a soldier asked them.

"Yes," one of the women said softly. "We ... we want to pray together."

"All right, just make it short," the soldier said.

The inhabitants of the Laotian town looked on; they would have liked to help, but could do nothing. Despite the severe pain in their bodies, the women said a faltering prayer. They tried to get up but fell back to the ground. Then one of them began singing in a shaky voice, "There is sunshine in my soul today...." The other nodded and tried to sing along.

Onlookers cried out "Save their lives! They are good people! They told us about Jesus!"

This infuriated the Vietnamese soldiers, and they

shouted to the people to keep quiet. Finally they aimed their rifles at the women and shot them through the head. They took the bodies, threw them in a wooden hut and set the hut on fire.

Yet, the death of these young women missionaries, who had only been in Indo-China for one year, was the start of a revival. Many Laotians in the town came to the knowledge of Jesus Christ.

"Truly, truly, I say to you, unless a grain of wheat falls into the earth and dies, it remains alone; but if it dies, it bears much fruit" (John 12:24). The blood of martyrs is still the seed of the Church.

The powers of darkness are getting ready for a last tremendous attack on the Church of Jesus Christ. Their most powerful weapon is to cripple us spiritually by disturbing our prayer times. They know they can freely attack Christians who do not pray. "Lord, teach us to pray."

If you want to work *for* God, you must appoint a committee. If you want to work *with* God, you must start a prayer group.

Chapter 11

## POINTS FOR PERSONAL REFLECTION

1. We are involved in a sipritual battle. Consider the description of Christ and Christians' foes in Ephesians 6:12. What does Colossians 2:15 have to say about their destiny?

2. Paul describes a spiritual "armor" in Ephesians 6:12-17. Can we use this armor ourselves?

3. In Ephesians 6:17-18, Paul describes two offensive weapons we can use. Jesus used them many times. Are you using them effectively?

4. A very practical illustration of the spiritual nature of human battles is recounted in Exodus 17:8-16. Moses, perhaps, was the key to victory, but Aaron and Hur

were absolutely essential; without them Joshua and his army coud have suffered defeat. Are any of these a model for the role you see you must play in Christ's kingdom?

## Chapter 12

# BEAR ONE ANOTHER'S BURDENS

The Suffering Church depends on our help. The Lord wants us to use our freedom to support those who have lost theirs. The Suffering Church has a special place with God.

"God has so composed the body, giving the greater honor to the inferior part" (1 Corinthians 12:24). The Church of Jesus Christ is called His body. It functions the same way as our own bodies. We see this clearly from sportsmen. If an athlete has a cold, he is unable to run. His head influences his legs and his whole body. He has to be in an optimal condition to give top performance. Just so with the Body of Christ. If one member suffers, the whole body suffers.

A Church which does not see the need of other Christians becomes so egocentric that it becomes ill because of it. Although the church visitation program may be good and the financial position sound, the spiritual level of the church will drop. A healthy church is the one which adopts a suffering church and helps it. "A liberal man will be enriched, and one who waters will himself be watered" (Proverbs 11:25).

If every Church which is free supports a church which is oppressed, the body of Christ will function better. It will create panic in hell but joy in heaven. We must be liberated from an introverted and self-sufficient Christianity which only revolves around itself. A Church which keeps rotating in its own circle impedes spiritual growth. In the meantime the Suffering Church is struggling alone in the battle when it desperately needs our help and love.

## How Are My Brothers?

Nehemiah in the Old Testament found himself in a difficult position. He had been taken into captivity. Yet, his thoughts constantly went out to those who were in more difficult circumstances. When one of his brothers, Hanani, visited him from Jerusalem, Nehemiah's first question was, "How are the others in Jerusalem?" He did not complain about his own situation. He wanted to know how his fellow citizens in Jerusalem were doing. He looked beyond his own problems to those whose problems were greater.

Are we prepared to inquire about the Suffering Church, or are we only interested in our own problems? The more we concern ourselves with our own problems, the bigger they grow. They result in self-pity and complaining.

Nehemiah wanted to know how the others were. The answer was not very encouraging: "The survivors there in the province who escaped exile are in great trouble and shame; the wall of Jerusalem is broken down, and its gates are destroyed by fire" (Nehemiah 1:3). It was a depressing report. Nehemiah was totally dismayed. "When I heard these words I sat down and wept, and mourned for days" (verse 4).

The answer to Nehemiah's question made him weep with sorrow. He was moved by the others' need. Whoever has come to know the Suffering Church will never be the same. The price those Christians pay for their faith is so great that you will never be able to free yourself from their need.

Yet, no help will go to the Suffering Church if we are only aware of the situation and mourn over it. Nehemiah knew that after learning of the situation he was also responsible to do something about it. The first question Nehemiah asked himself after he had heard of their problems was, "What can I do?" He then proceeded to fast and pray. He identified himself with his suffering associates: "Yea, I and my father's house have sinned" (verse 6). Nehemiah knew he was not better or more saintly than the others.

As we view the situation of the Suffering Church and see how many nations have lost their freedom, we might ask, "Why do they suffer and not we? Is that the reason we still live in freedom?" If we are honest before the Lord, we will, with Nehemiah, confess, "Yea, I and my father's house have sinned."

We are no better than the one thousand million Chinese or the three hundred million Russians. Why then does God give us freedom? Because we are better Christians? No, we also are guilty before God. If the Lord had to look upon the sins in our land, then we should be punished. Yet God does not do it — not yet. I believe He gives us freedom so that we may be able to use it in the interests of His Kingdom — to enable us to help His suffering body and so "bear one another's burdens."

After his confession, Nehemiah made plans to help his suffering fellow citizens. He went back to Jerusalem and, under difficult circumstances, rebuilt the wall. The opposition was great, but Nehemiah was determined to execute the order he had accepted: "The God of heaven will make us prosper, and we his servants will arise and build" (Nehemiah 2:20).

## An Open Door

More than twenty-five years ago Brother Andrew visited Eastern Europe for the first time. He saw how thousands of young Polish Communists marched across a square and called out, "We are poor, but we will conquer the world!" Their dedication to a godless revolution was evident. The Lord spoke to him: "If they think they can conquer the world without Me, how much more can My people do it with Me!"

Brother Andrew read the words of Revelation 3:2, "Awake, and strengthen what remains and is on the point of death." That was the birth of Open Doors. He devoted his life to strengthening the Suffering Church from that day. He soon got in touch with Christians in Eastern Europe and asked what he could do for them. The answer was always the same: "Send us Bibles."

He returned to Holland and used the little amount of money he had to buy Bibles. Then, in a donated Volkswagen, he returned to Eastern Europe. His small car was laden with Bibles. Would the customs officers discover and seize the Bibles? Before crossing the border Brother Andrew prayed, "Lord, I have Your Word for Your children. Don't let the customs find them. When You were on earth, You opened the eyes of the blind. Now please blind the eyes of the customs guards."

The Lord heard his prayer — again and again. Now twenty-five years later, hundreds of teams regularly go to Eastern Europe, China, Mozambique, etc. Thousands of Bibles cross the borders daily, and God protects His people and His Word.

The Lord gave us an open door which no one can shut.

I discussed in an earlier chapter why we take in Bibles this way. The few Bibles which Communist governments import legally, now and then, are by far not enough for all the Christians. Also it is compulsory in many countries for an individual to register his name when he purchases a legally imported Bible (chapter 4). Our organization tries to make it possible for them to receive a Bible without having to divulge their names to the authorities.

We do not want to defend this method of taking in Bibles against those who continuously maintain that "smuggling" is unnecessary. Nehemiah inevitably received opposition and criticism of his method of work; his opponents repeatedly accused him of illegal work (Nehemiah 2:19, chapters 4 and 6). He did not see the necessity of debate or self-defense. His answer was simply, "I am doing a great work" (Nehemiah 6:3), and he continued. As long as there are millions of Christians in Communist countries who do not possess a Bible, we will continue with this great work.

### The Reaction of the Suffering Church

My first visit to a Communist country was an unforgettable experience. After a journey of more than six hundred miles, I arrived at the house of a Christian in Hungary. We drove into the garage of this brother and he

immediately locked the door behind us. He kissed the
Bible when I handed it to him. Then he came to me and
embraced me. He was astonished when I told him that I
had brought a thousand Bibles. He could not believe his
ears. "My congregation will be very happy,' he said ex-
citedly.

As we were stacking the Bibles, he asked whether I
had any Romanian Bibles as well. I told him I had brought
a hundred with me. "Why are you so anxious for
Romanian Bibles?" I asked.

"Because six months ago a brother from Romania
visited me," he replied. "He is a member of a secret
church and has been unable to get Bibles. He was hoping
that I would be able to get some for him in this country. I
told him I would do all I could to help him. Now I will be
able to give him a hundred Bibles when he comes again!"

We carried on unpacking when suddenly we heard a
knock at the garage door. Startled, the brother said
softly, "Police!" I was frightened out of my wits and
looked about me. Everywhere were Bibles. It would be
impossible to hide them fast enough.

"Keep quiet and remain here," the brother said. "I will
go outside and see who it is."

He switched off the light and disappeared into an ante-
room which had a staircase leading outside. I stayed in
the darkness, perspiring with anxiety. What did the
police want? Had they followed me? The brother stayed
away for a few minutes. Eventually the door opened; he
switched on the light and walked toward me. I saw he was
crying.

With my last bit of courage I stood up and said, "It is all
right, brother, I am willing to go with you to the police."

He stood in front of me, shaking his head, momentarily
unable to speak because of the emotion. Finally, through
his tears, he stammered, "It is not the police. It is . . . it is
the brother from Romania! He is back!"

"The one who asked for the Bibles?" I exclaimed with
astonishment.

"Yes," the brother said, wiping his eyes. "How is it
possible? O God, You are so good!"

My Hungarian friend and I gathered as many Bibles

together as our arms would hold and together we went to the next room where the Romanian was. I went over to him and handed him the Bibles. The man looked at me, then at the Bibles. Lifting up his hands, he cried out, "O Jesus, Jesus, thank you — at last!"

Afterward we all embraced and thanked the Lord.

## Angels of God

Today Africa is the major battlefield of revolution. Some countries already have a Communist government. Other countries are threatened. The first to suffer are the Christians. Evangelizing has been forbidden. Christians who do witness openly are persecuted. Bibles are scarce.

This is one of the reasons Open Doors maintains a work to help the Suffering Church in Africa. Just as in Europe and in Asia, there is a great need for the Word of God.

A while ago we received a request from Mozambique to take Bibles into that country. We were dubious at first because we were under the impression that Bibles were still available there. This was true; Maputo did receive consignments now and then. The demand was so great, however, that within a few days the Bibles were sold out. Many Christians traveled to Maputo hoping there would still be a few copies left.

In the north of Mozambique there are thousands of Christians. They also want God's Word and have tried in Beira, the second largest city in Mozambique, to buy Bibles. However, no Bibles were to be found.

We sent a few teams to Maputo to buy any Bibles that were available. They returned with four Portuguese Bibles; there were no more. We then decided to help the churches in northern Mozambique by smuggling in Bibles.

One of our teams had an exceptional experience. They were en route to a certain small church when they were arrested by Frelimo soldiers. Fortunately they could hide the Bibles. They were kept in custody for three days and interrogated. After that they were released and ordered to return to their own country (in mid-Africa). The two couriers left the village and made as if to return to their own country. But by the way of a detour they returned to the cache of Bibles, for they did not want to return home until they had delivered them.

That afternoon they were arrested again by a Frelimo soldier. He pointed to the box and wanted to know its contents. They had no alternative but to open it. He looked at the Bibles and then at the two Christians and said, "We try to do everything in our power to prevent this book from being imported. You must really love the Bible to risk your life twice."

The Lord softened his heart, and the two young Christians witnessed fervently about their faith in Jesus Christ. Finally they gave him a Bible. He accepted it and said, "Now I know that your God is a God of love to send you here with Bibles for the Christians." Then he let them go. In one hand he held his gun; in the other he held the Sword of the Spirit: the Bible.

The two Christians eventually reached their destination. What great joy filled the small congregation when they saw the Bibles! The minister expressed the thoughts of his congregation: "Thank you for coming. We felt so forsaken. Now we know you really love us and think of us."

They shared the Bibles with all the hungry Christians; then the team returned home. They took a different route to the border and met little groups of Christians along the way. The highlight of their journey was meeting an elderly brother. He was pastor of a church, but even he didn't have a Bible.

"What do you preach from?" asked one of the couriers.

The man went into a nearby house and returned with an old hymnbook. The pages were torn and yellow. "From this," he said. "It is all I have. The hymns speak of the love of God and I preach about it."

The couriers felt so sorry for him and offered to have his old hymnbook reprinted, if he would let them take the book back with them. The old man shook his head. Pressing the yellowed pages to his breast, he said, "If I give it away, I have nothing at all."

One of the couriers took his personal Bible and said, "I

will give you my Bible for your hymnbook, so that we can take it and have it reprinted for you."

The man looked at the young Christian in surprise. "A real Bible for my hymnbook?"

As he handed over the hymnbook, he accepted the Bible, and his eyes shone as he opened the Word of God. Behind him stood the other Christians; they also wanted Bibles. He saw the longing in their eyes, looked at the two couriers and said, "Angels of God, if I go with you, can I have more Bibles for my church?"

They invited him to come along, and a week later the old brother returned with a case full of Bibles, to the great joy of the Christians in his town.

## Eat, Drink and Share

When the wall of Jerusalem was built, the Jews celebrated that great occasion (Nehemiah 8). They had every reason to do so. From then on they would be safe against any outside attacks.

Nehemiah, however, was not happy with the attitude of the celebrating multitudes. He noticed that they were only thinking about themselves. He conveyed a principle to them which he himself had learned. They could celebrate, but at the same time they were to remember those who were not as privileged as they: "Go your way, eat the fat and drink sweet wine and send portions to him for whom nothing is prepared" (Nehemiah 8:10).

This principle was characteristic of Nehemiah. He thought not only of himself but also about others. His greatest joy was to help others who had bigger problems than himself.

We can learn much from him. Many of us have perhaps never had to endure persecution. We may rejoice and thank God for that fact. At the same time we are called to think of those who have lost their freedom. We may not be selfish and think about our own welfare only.

"Let each of you look not only to his own interests, but also the interests of others" (Philippians 2:4).

Whoever wants to prepare for future persecution will

get great blessing out of the principle of Nehemiah 8:12:
*"Eat, drink and share!"*

Chapter 12

## POINTS FOR PERSONAL REFLECTION

1. In Hebrews 13:1-3, there are commands given that relate directly to our responsibility for the Suffering
   Church. How is it possible to remember prisoners and
   others who suffer as if we "were there with them?"

2. How can we relate Paul's statements in 2 Corinthians
   8:13-15 to our responsibility for care and love for the
   Suffering Church and to their responsibility to us? For
   an answer to the second half of the question, see
   2 Corinthians 9:12-15.

3. Are you personally involved in assistance to the
   Suffering Church? Do you intend to be? How?

A challenging and informative group Bible study supplement to this book is available from Open Doors. For each copy, send $1.25 to:

Open Doors With Brother Andrew
P.O. Box 2020
Orange, California 92669

You can share in Open Doors' ministry to the Suffering Church through prayer, giving and sharing the need with others. For more information, write the Open Doors office nearest you.

CANADA: Open Doors With Brother Andrew
P.O. Box 61, Station D
Toronto, Ontario M6P 3J5, Canada

AUSTRALIA: Open Doors With Brother Andrew
P.O. Box 724, Crows Nest
NSW 2065, Australia

NEW ZEALAND: Open Doors With Brother Andrew
P.O. Box 6123
Auckland 1, New Zealand

ENGLAND: Open Doors With Brother Andrew
P.O. Box 6, Standlake, Witney
Oxon OX8 7SH, England

PHILIPPINES: Open Doors With Brother Andrew
P.O. Box 4282
Manila, Philippines

SOUTH AFRICA: Open Doors With Brother Andrew
P.O. Box 990099
Kibler Park
2053 Johannesburg, South Africa

HOLLAND: Open Doors With Brother Andrew
P.O. Box 47
3850AA Ermelo, Holland